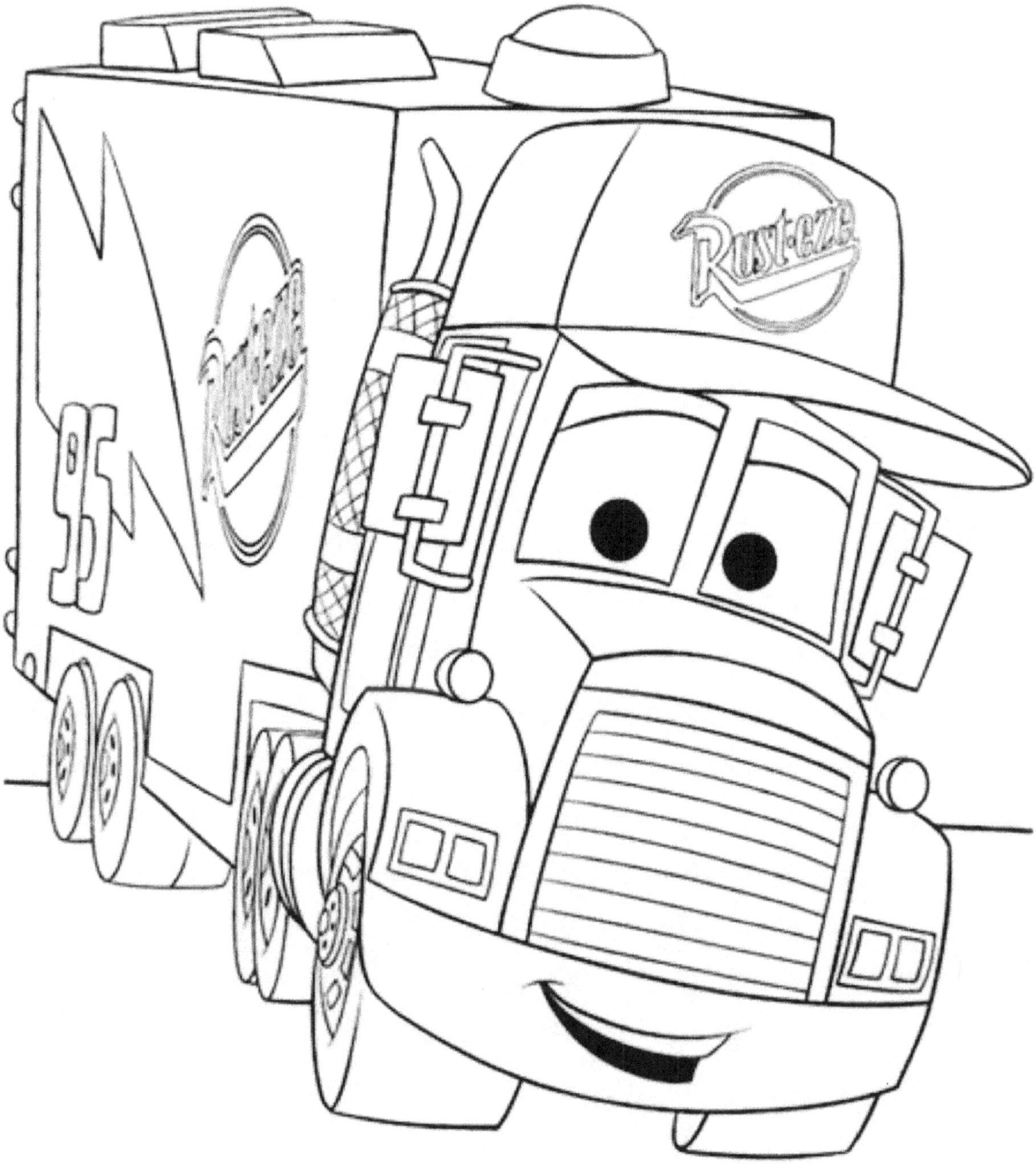
Rust-eze
95

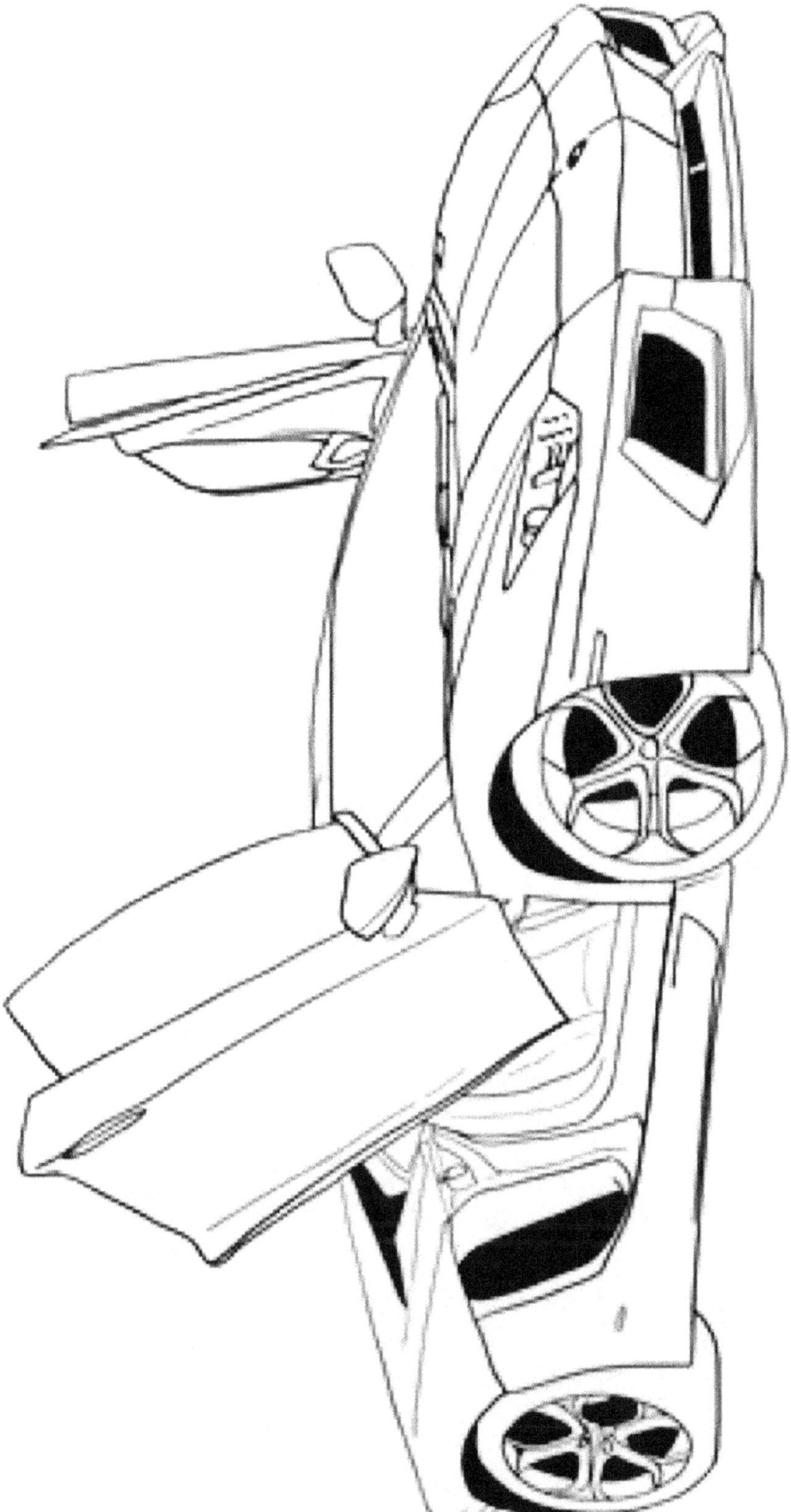

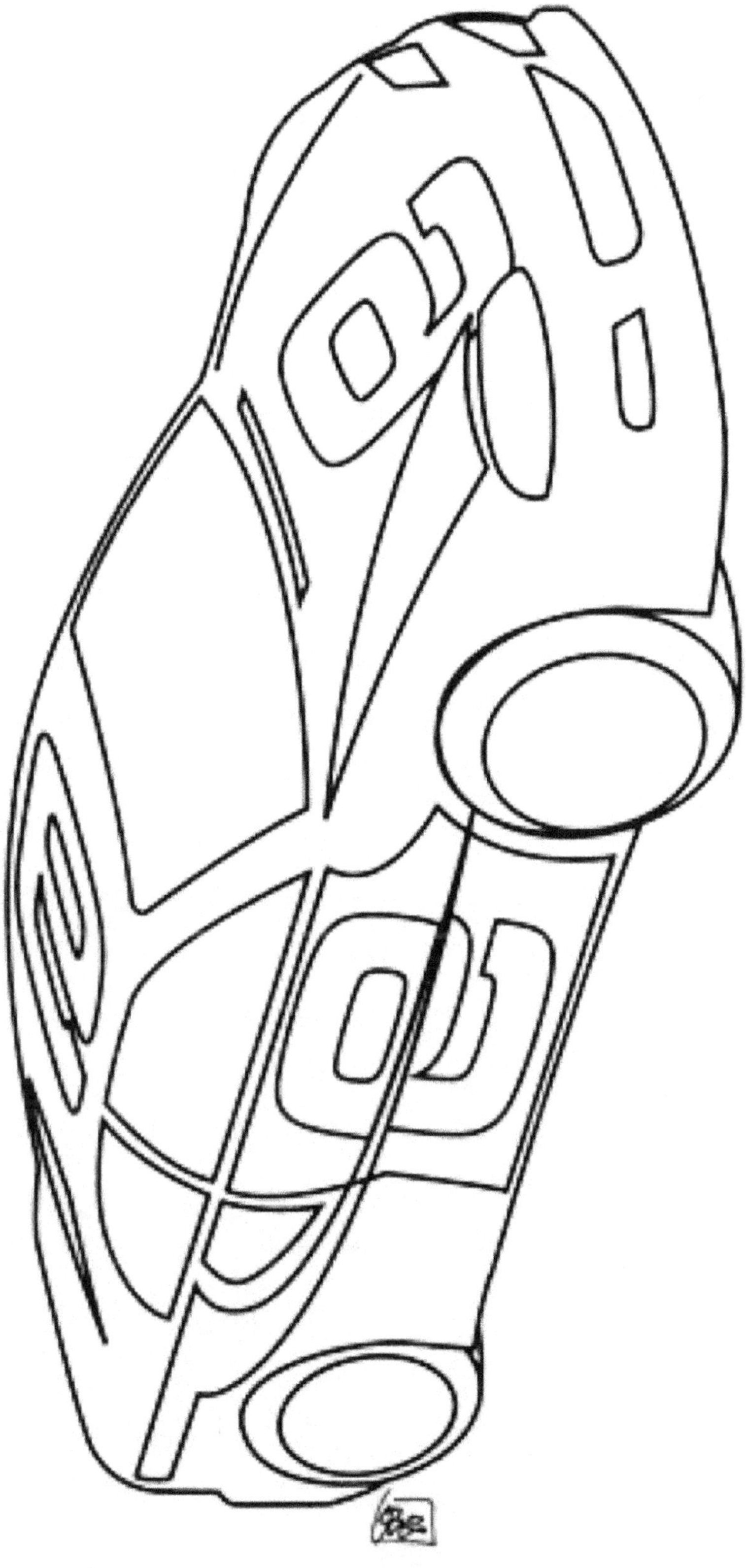

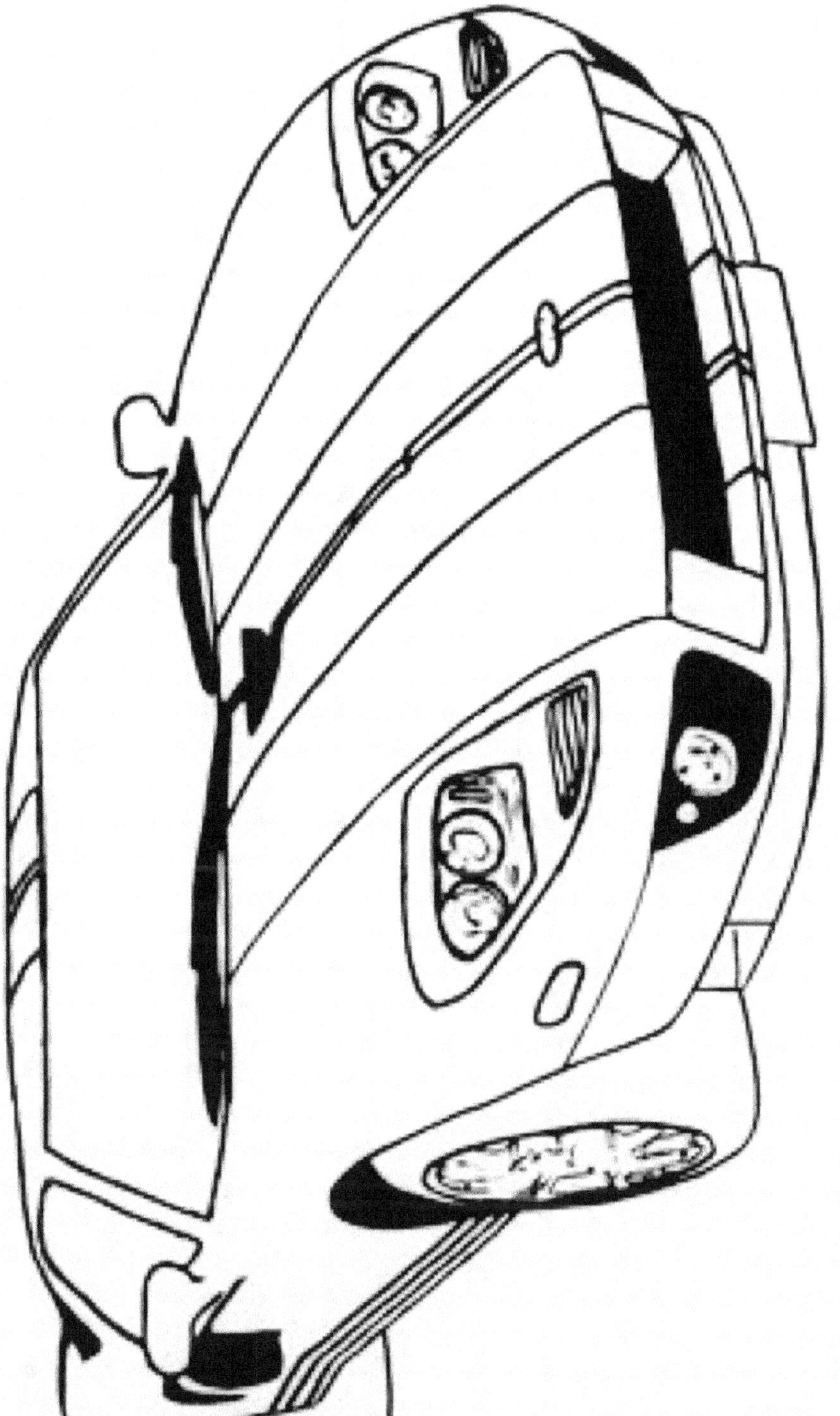

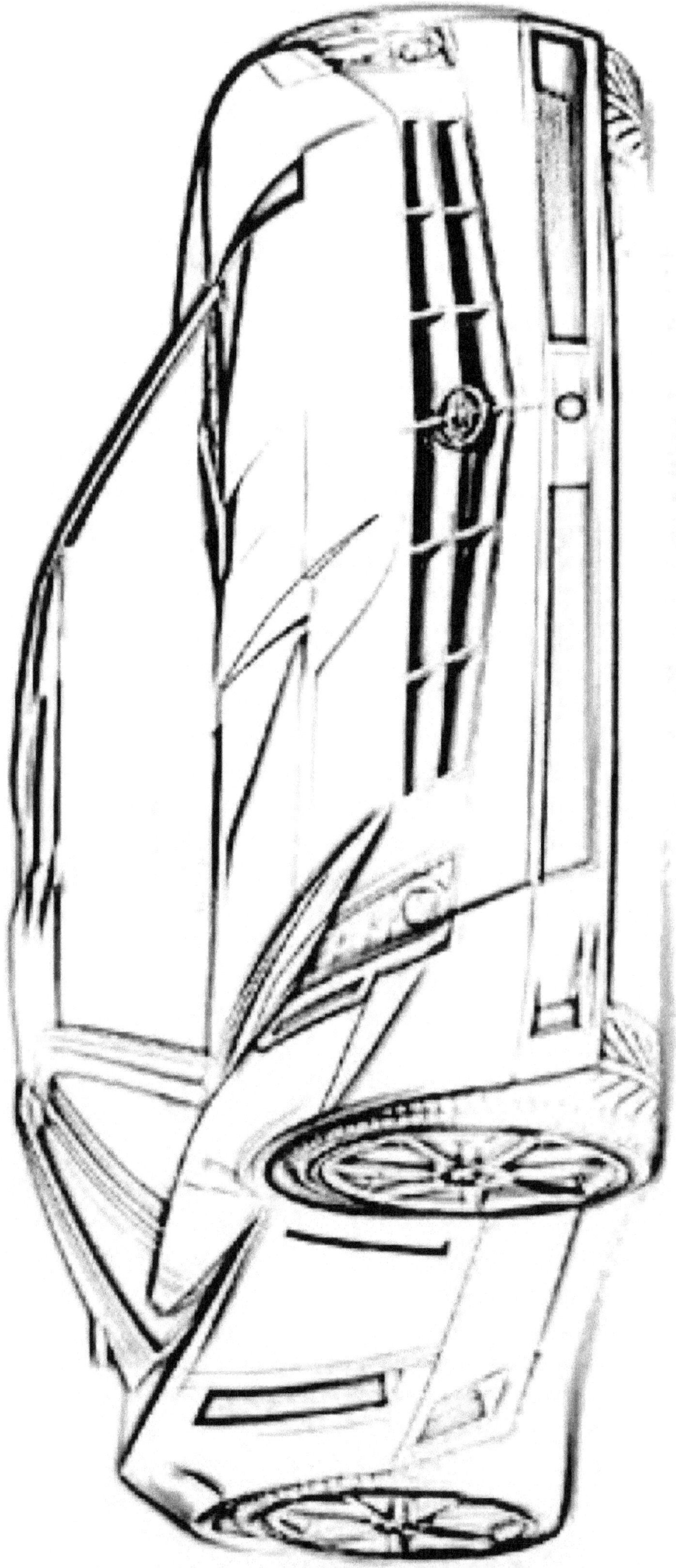

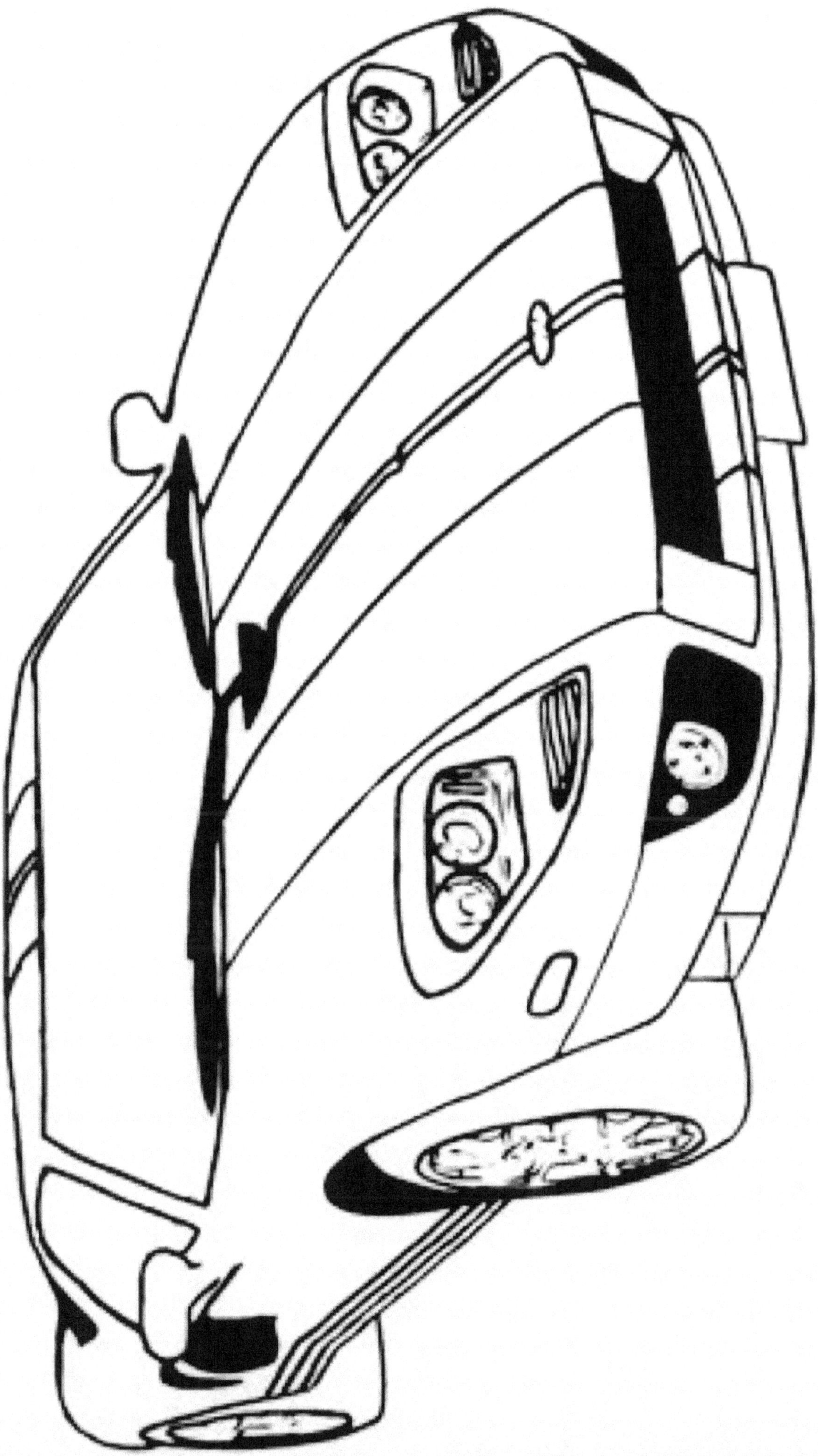

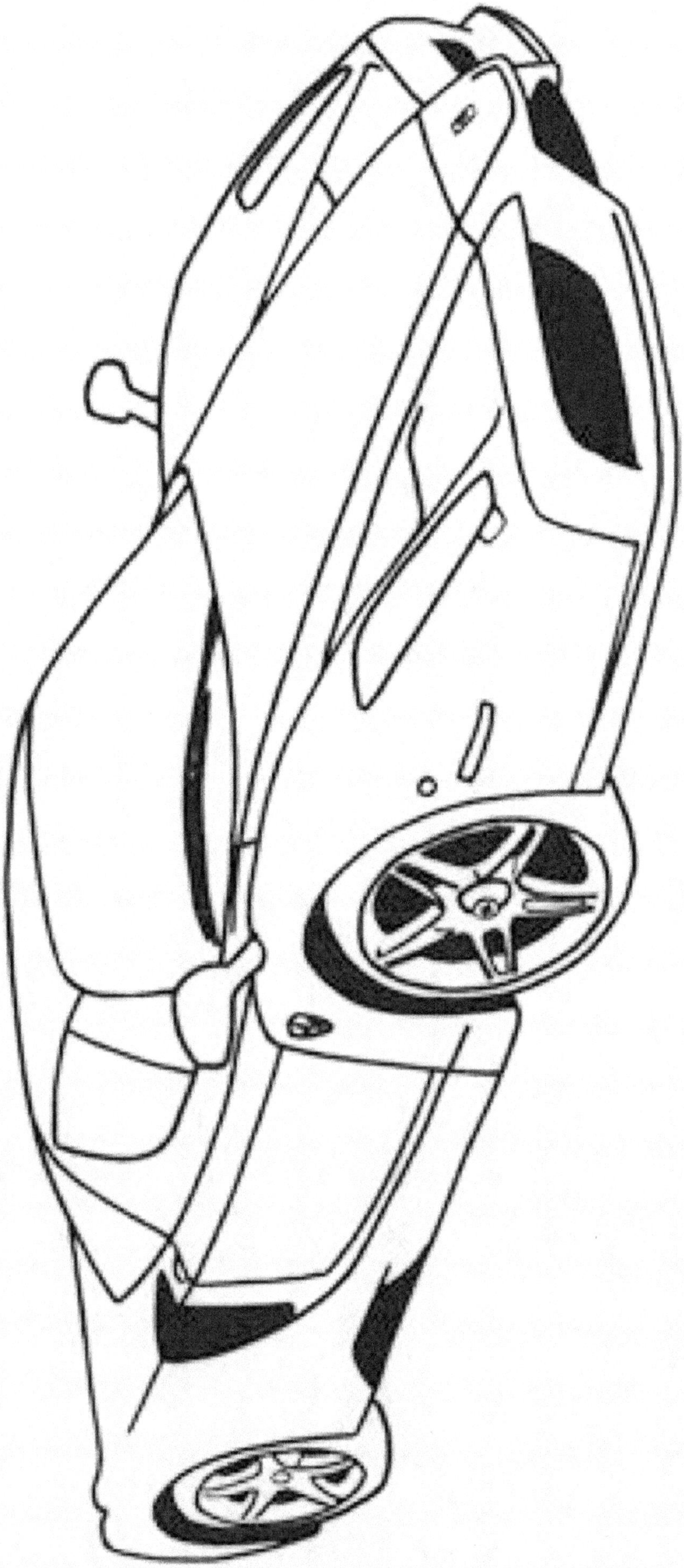

Simple Car

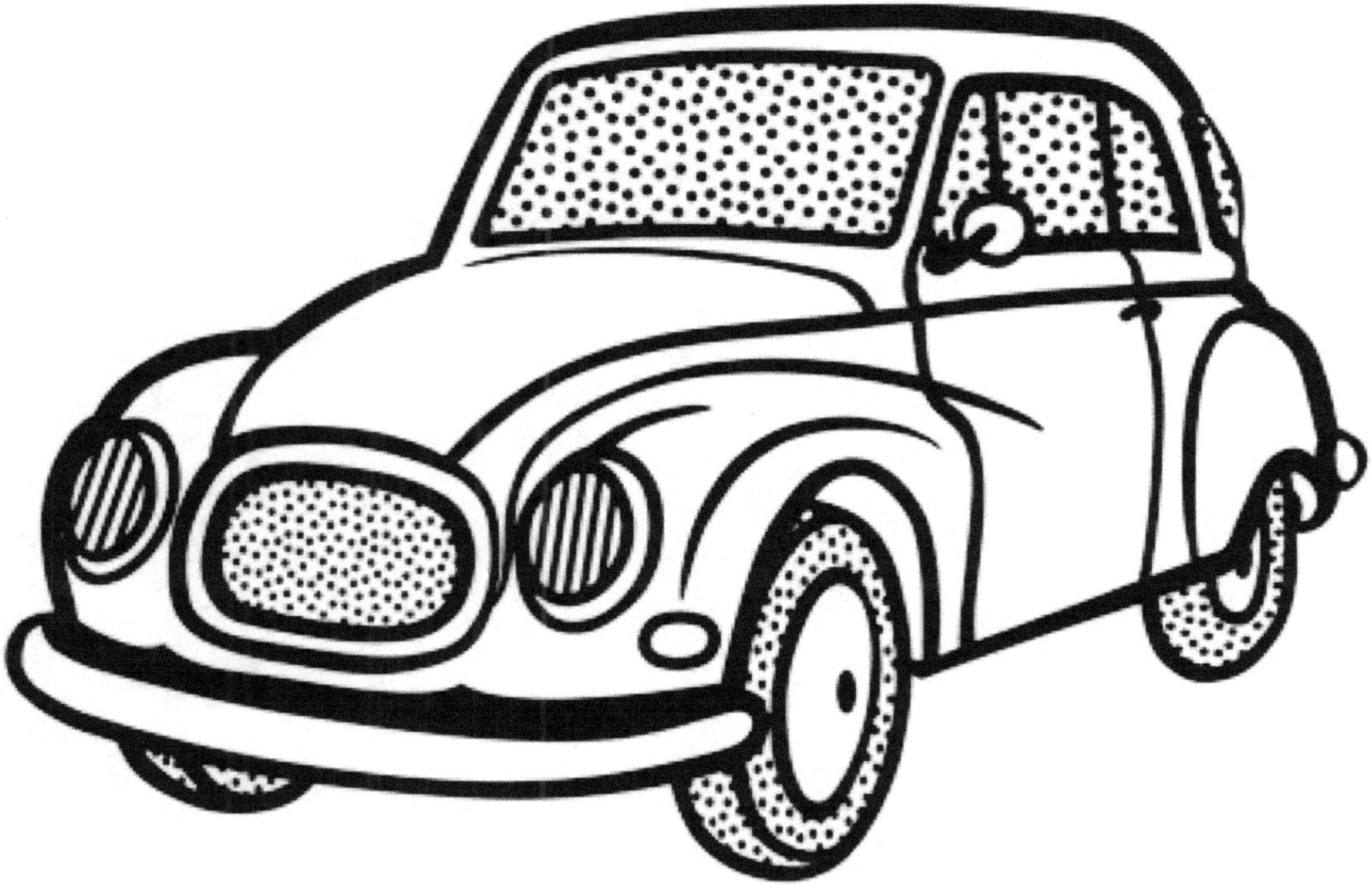

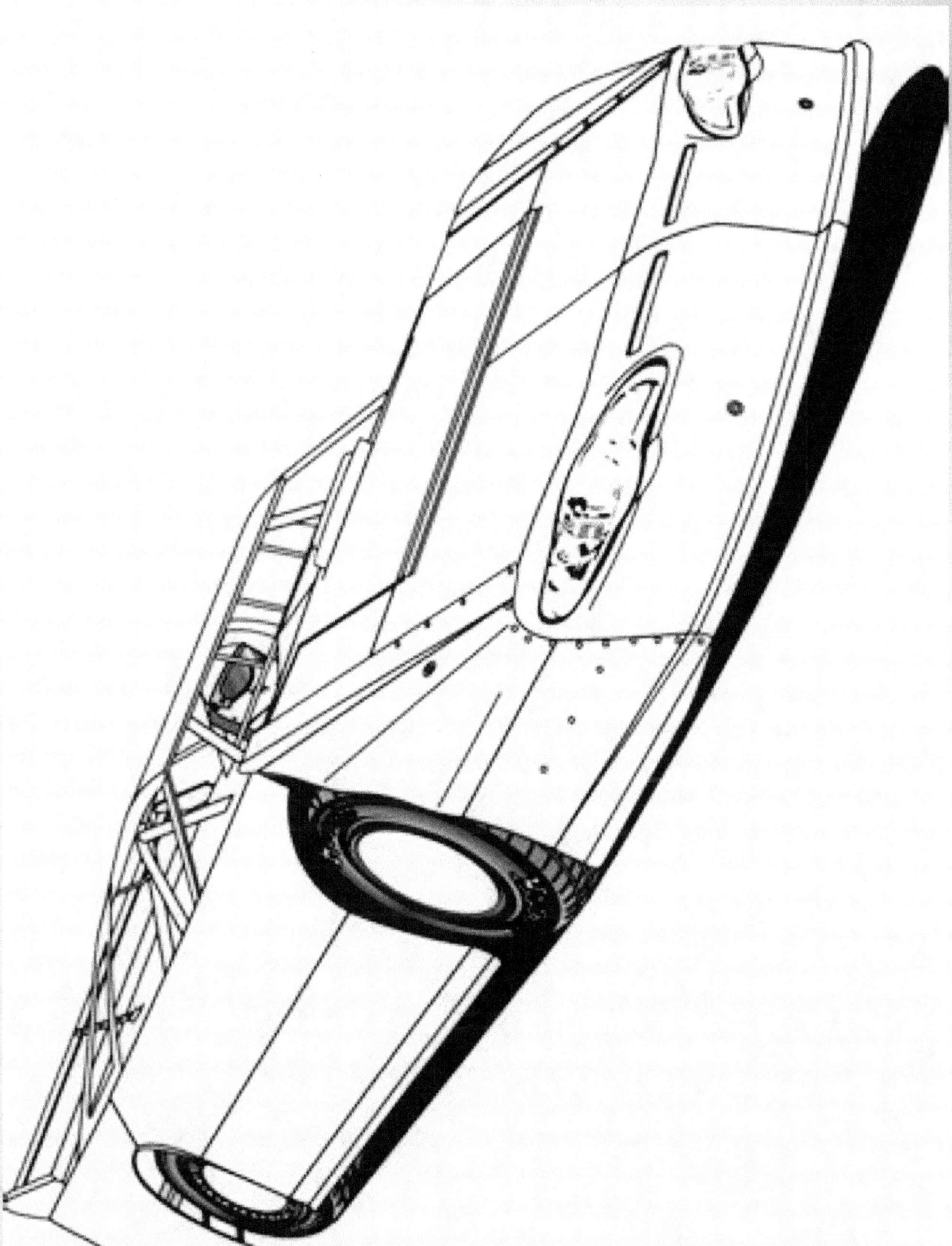

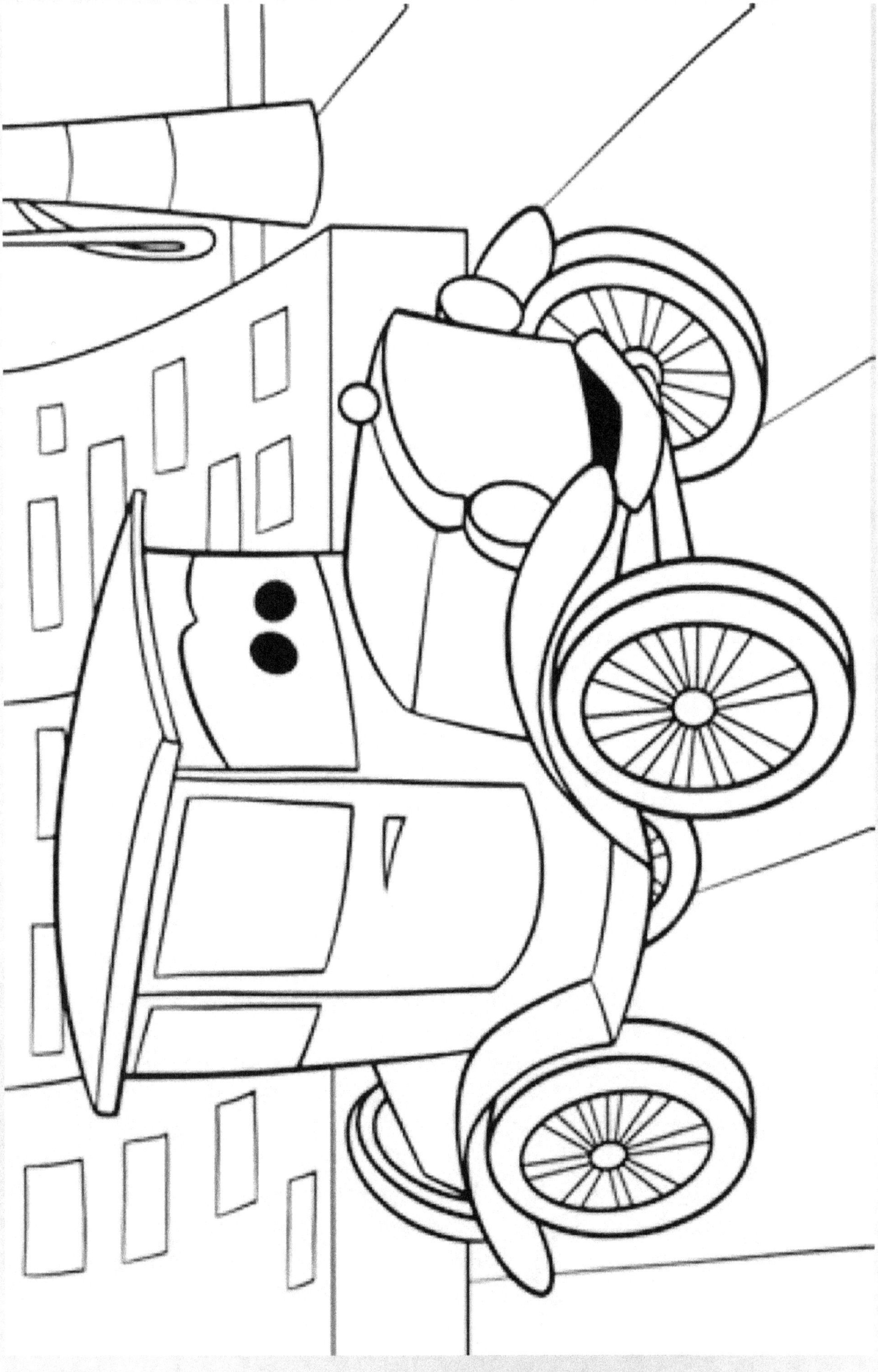

Sports Car

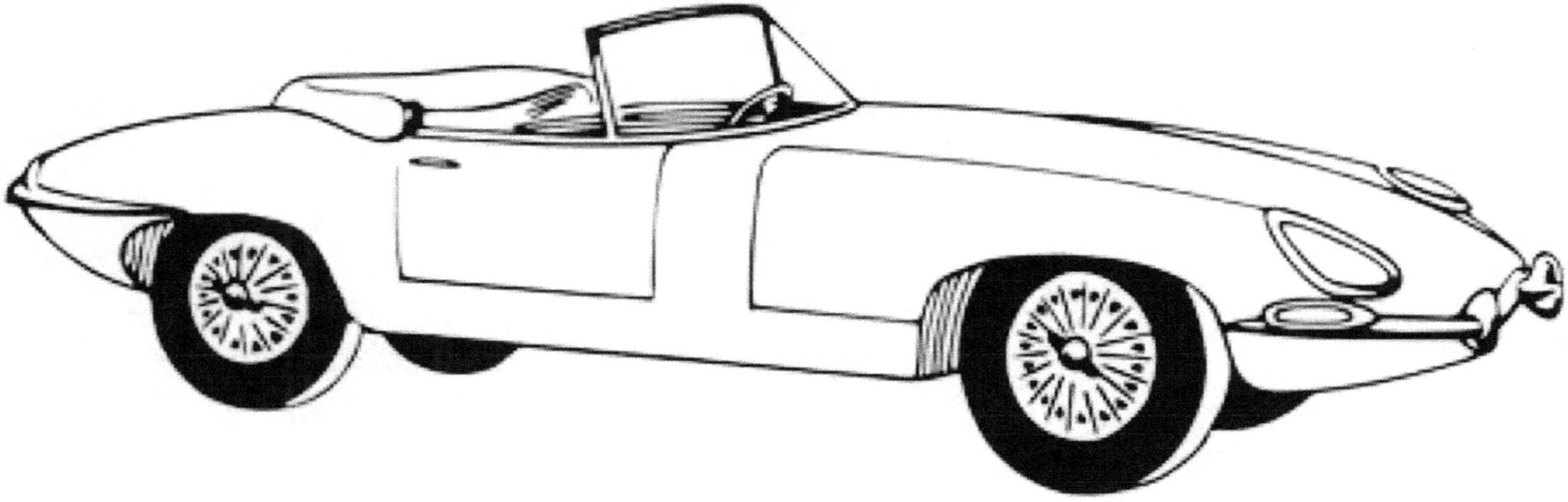

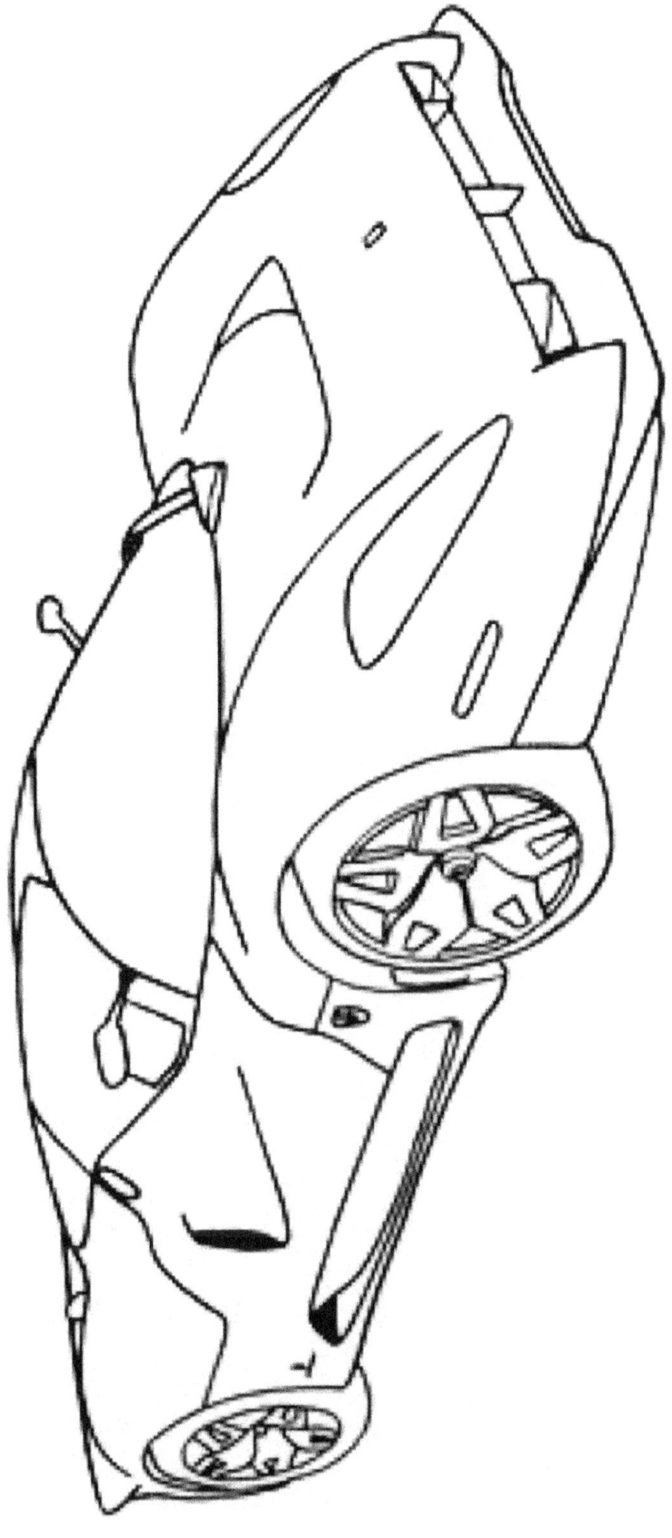

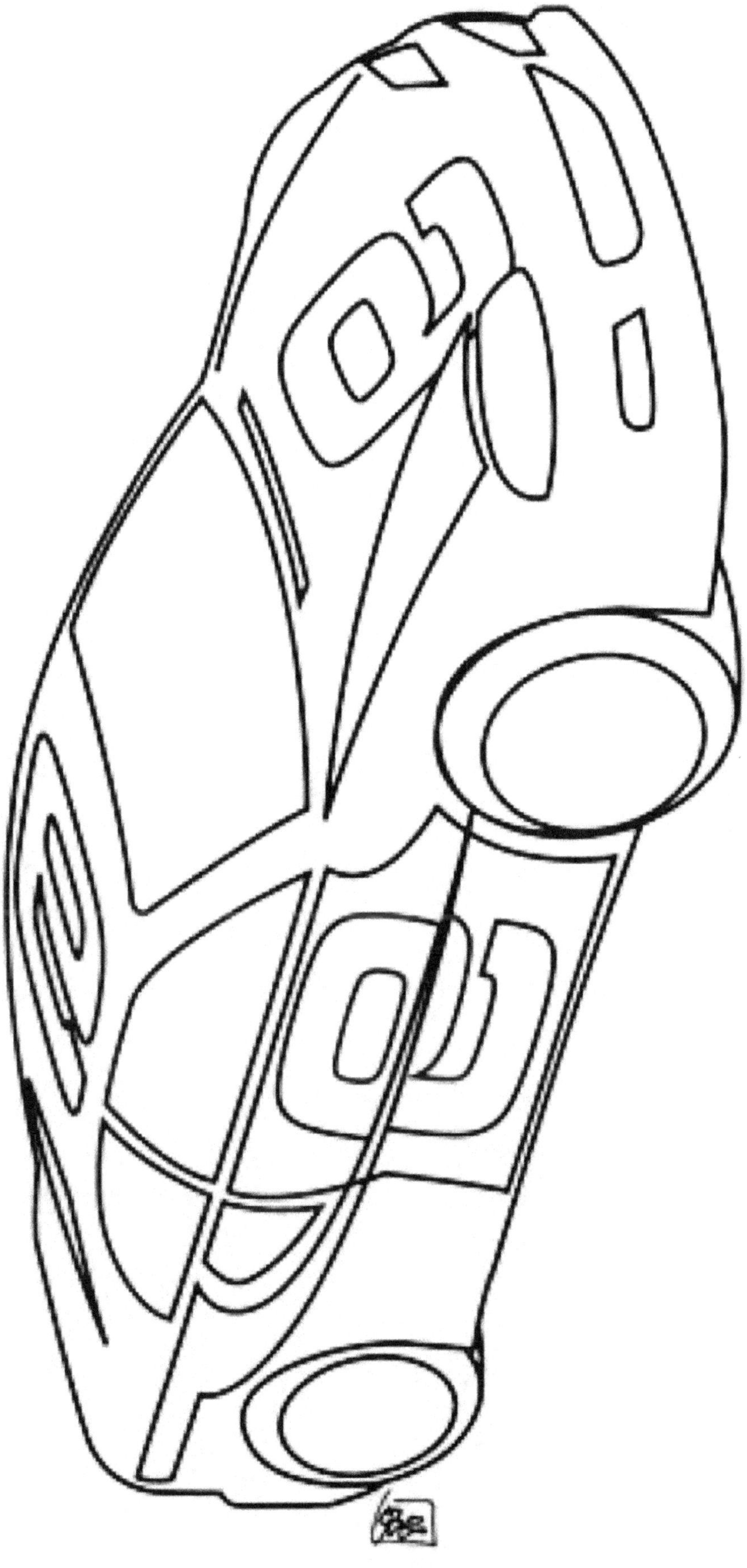

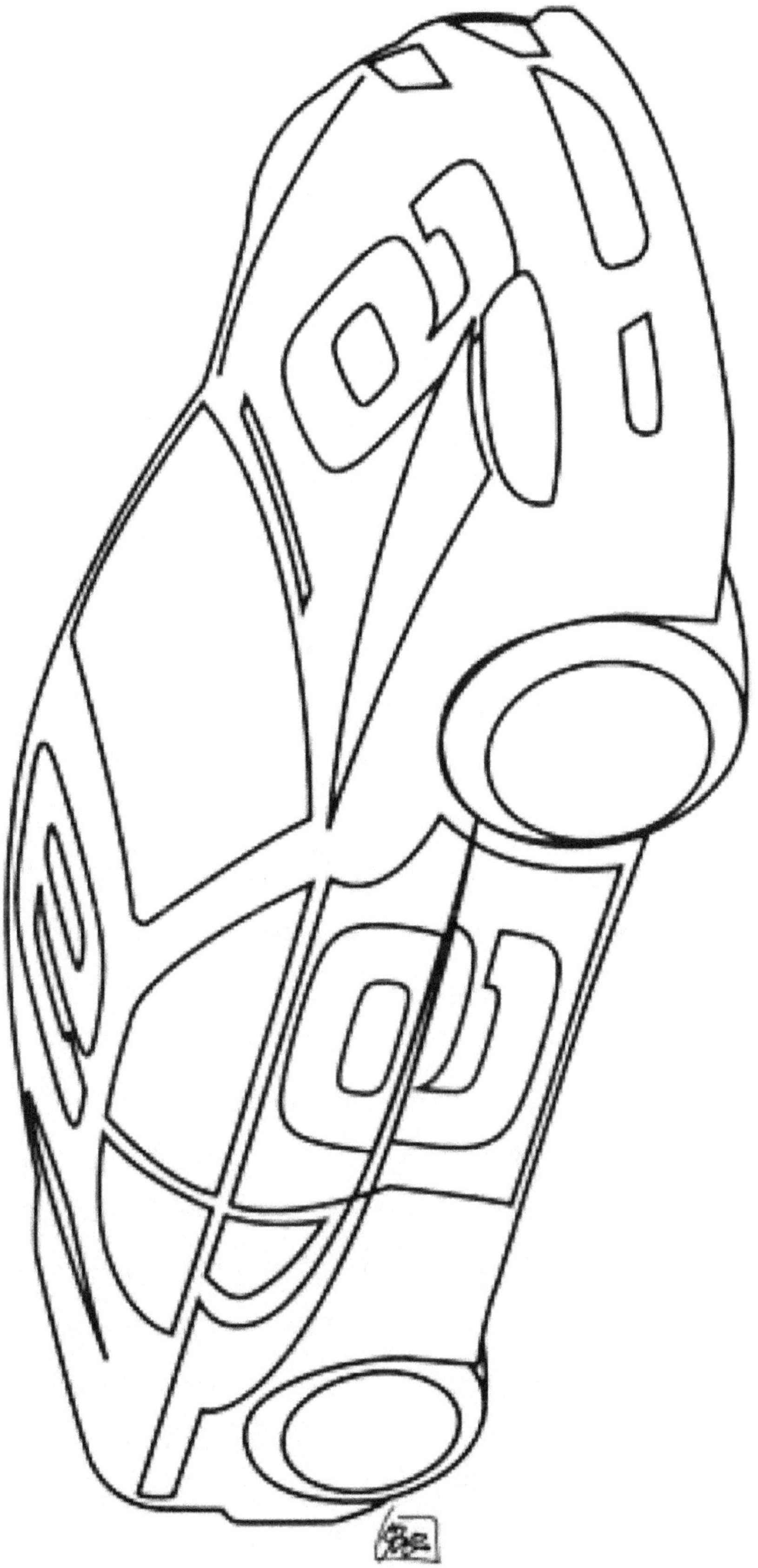

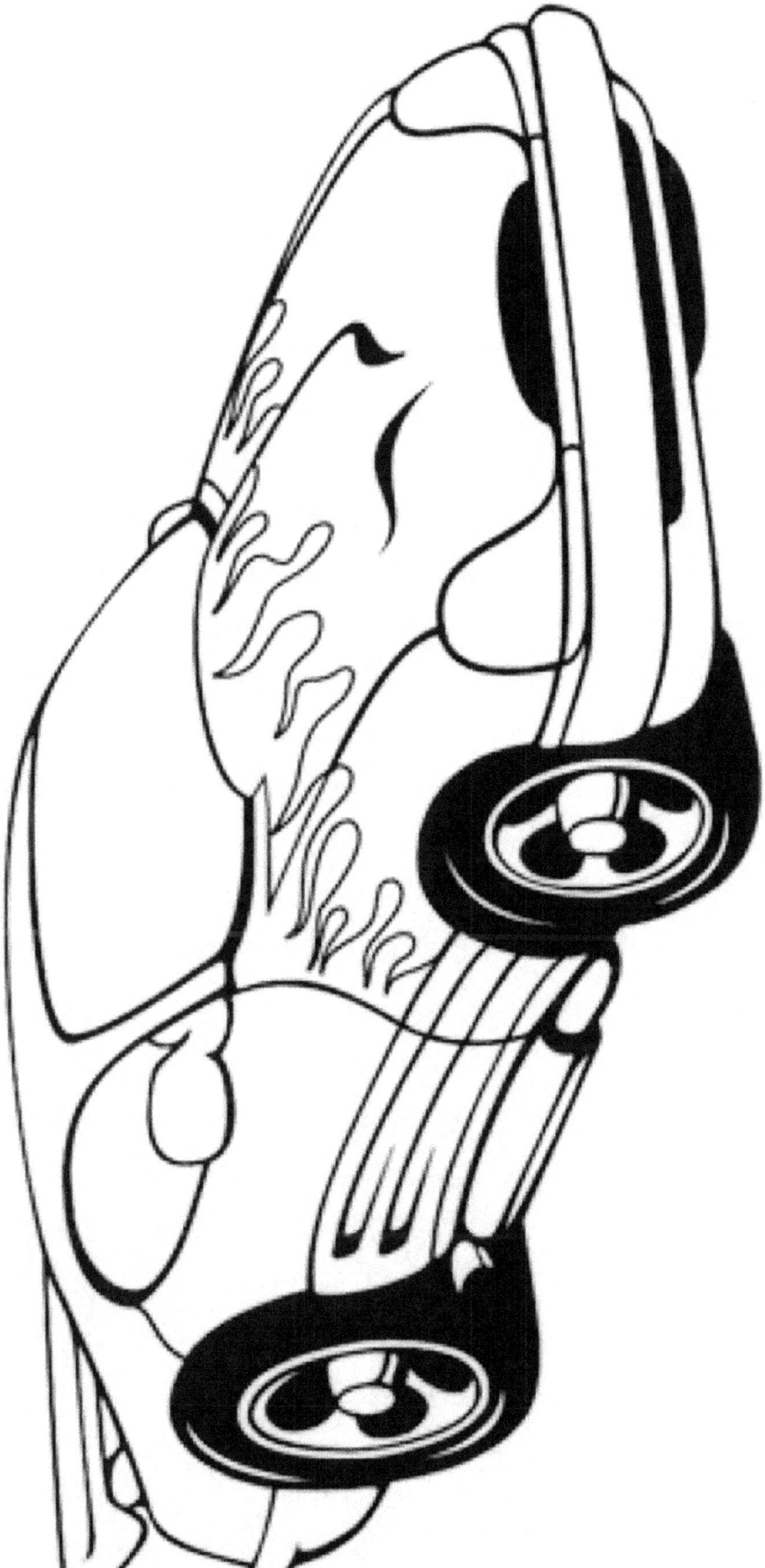

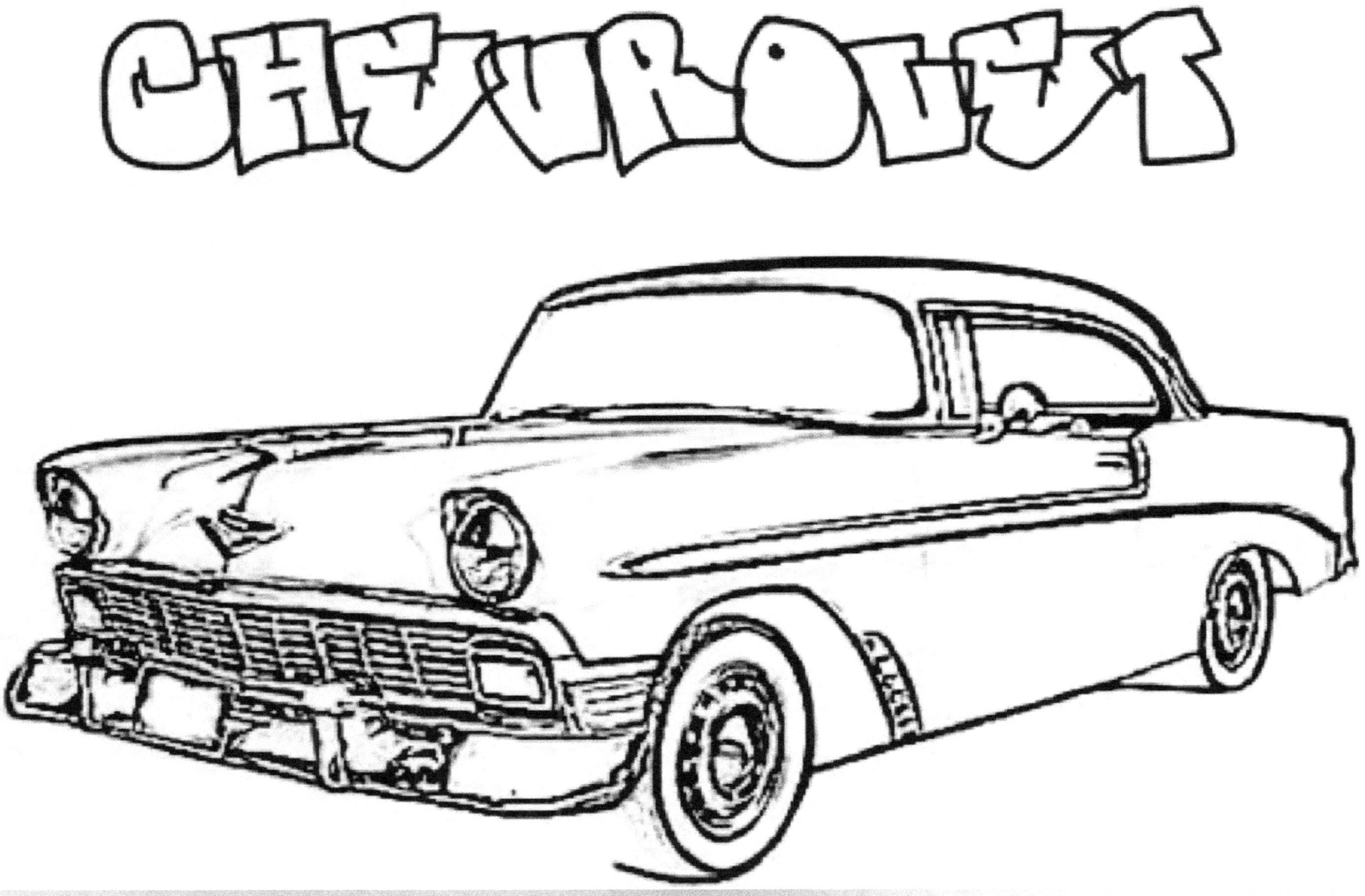
CHEVROLET

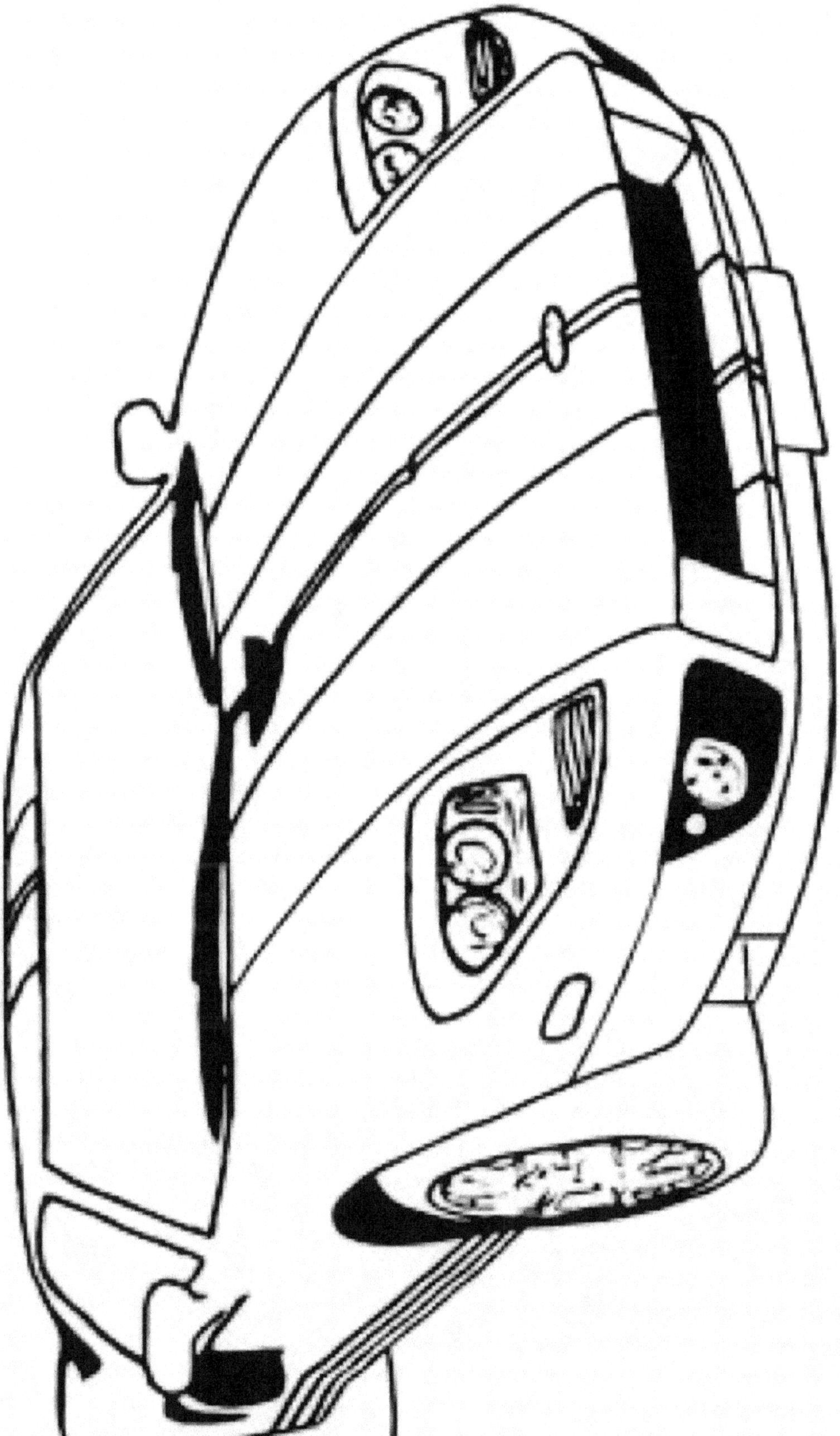

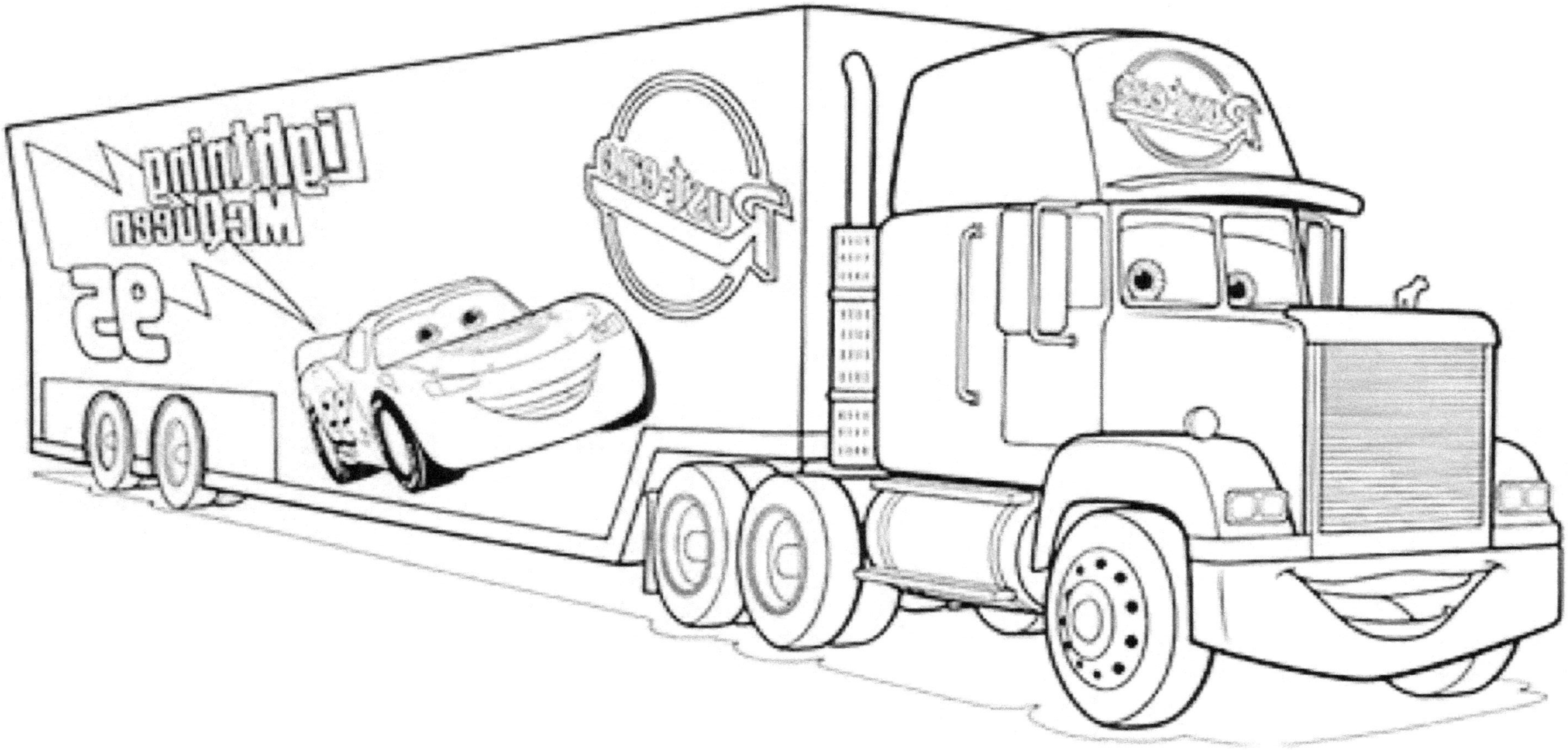
Rust-eze
Lightning McQueen
95

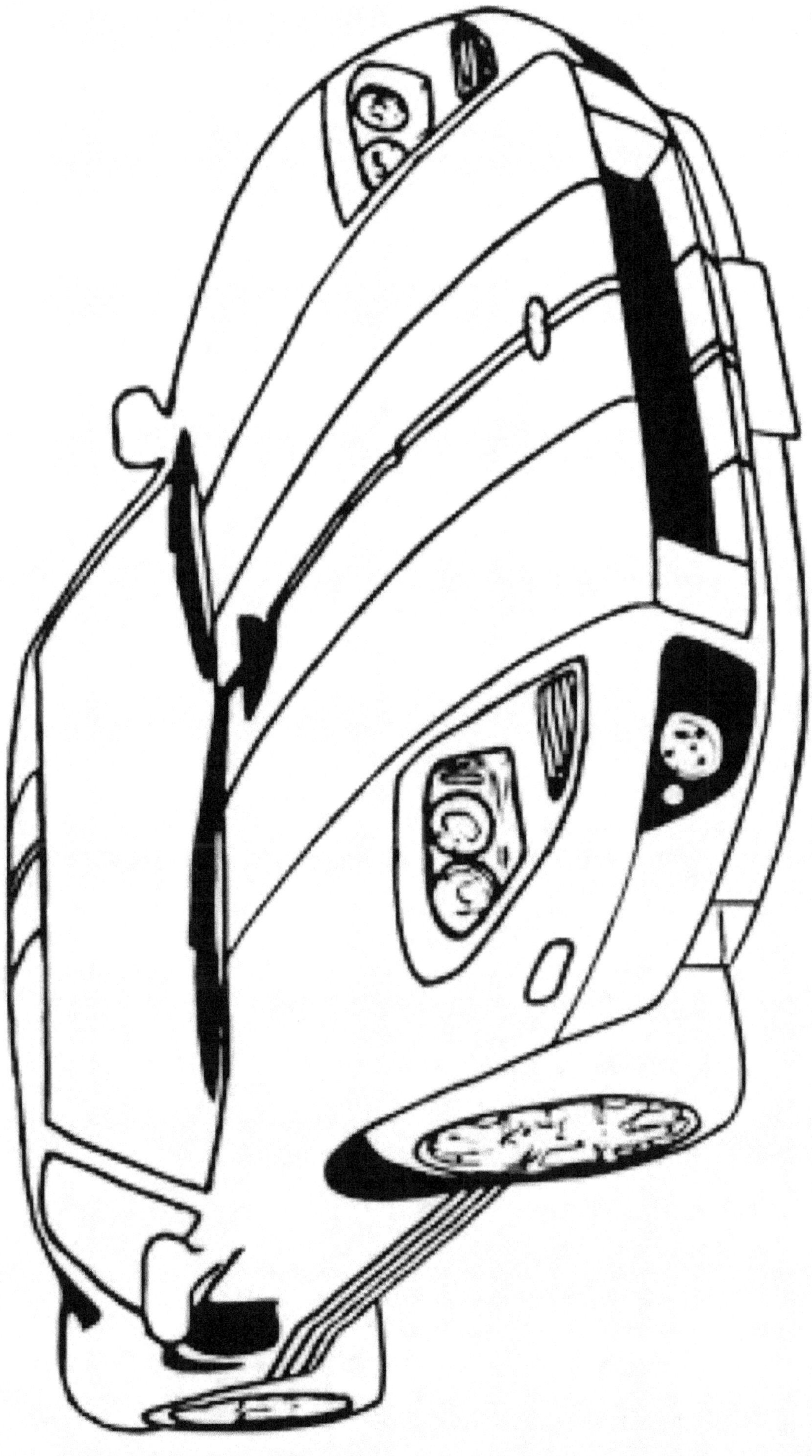

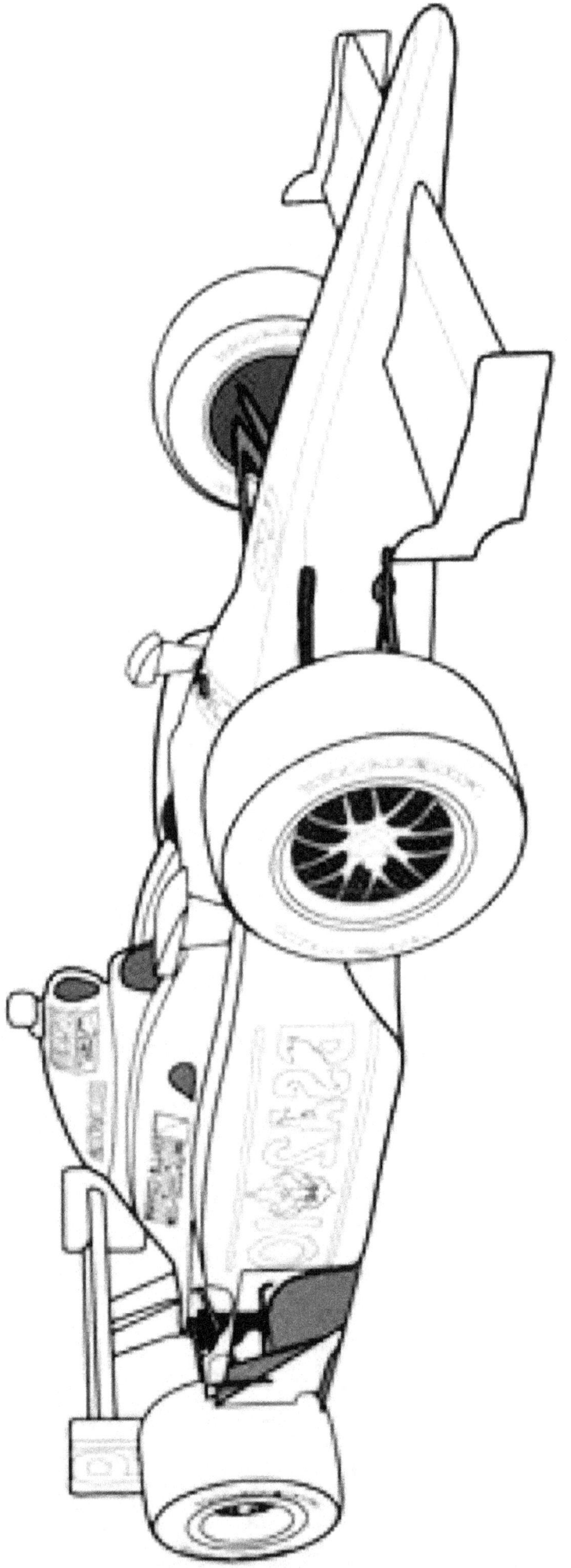

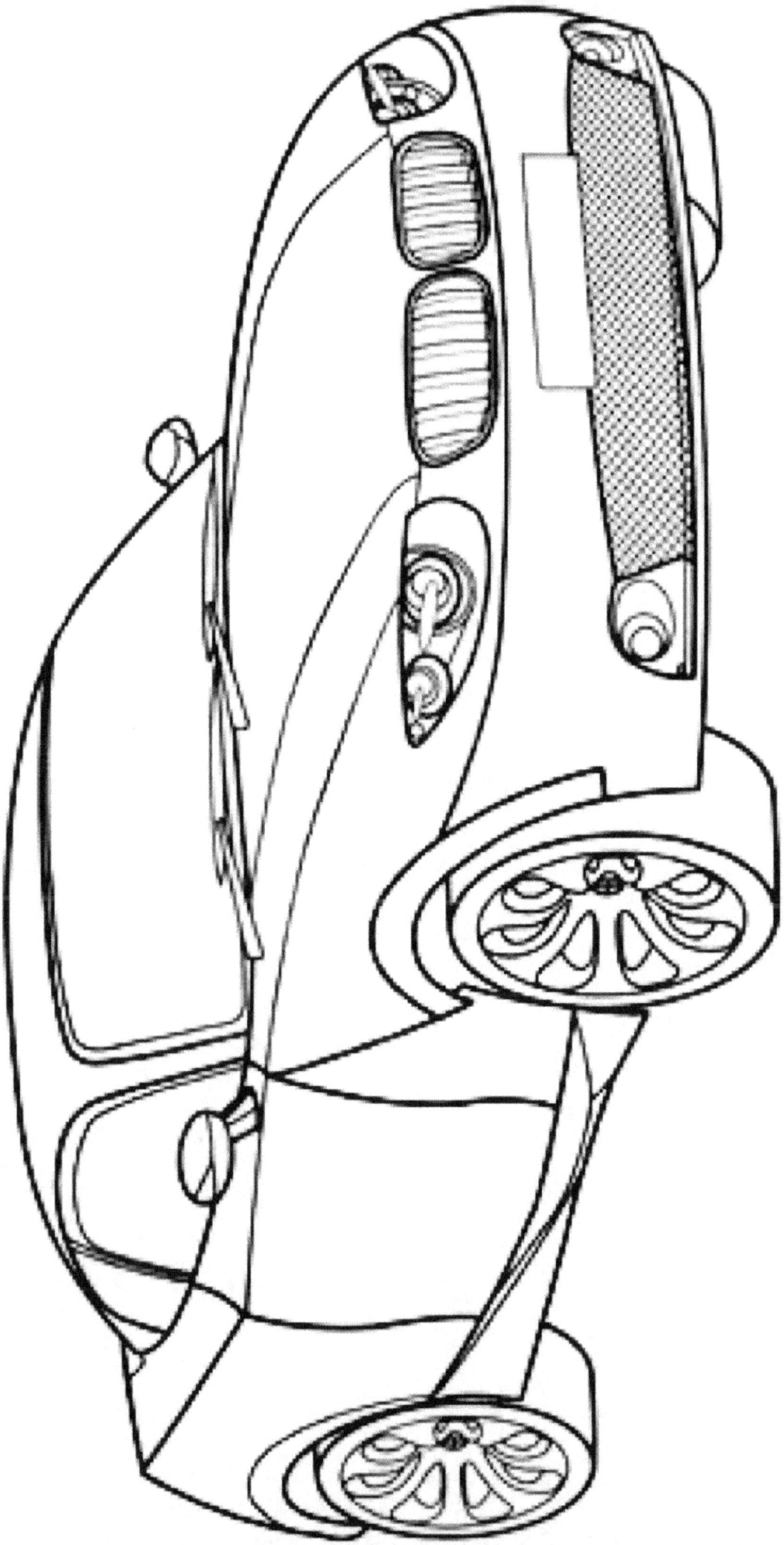

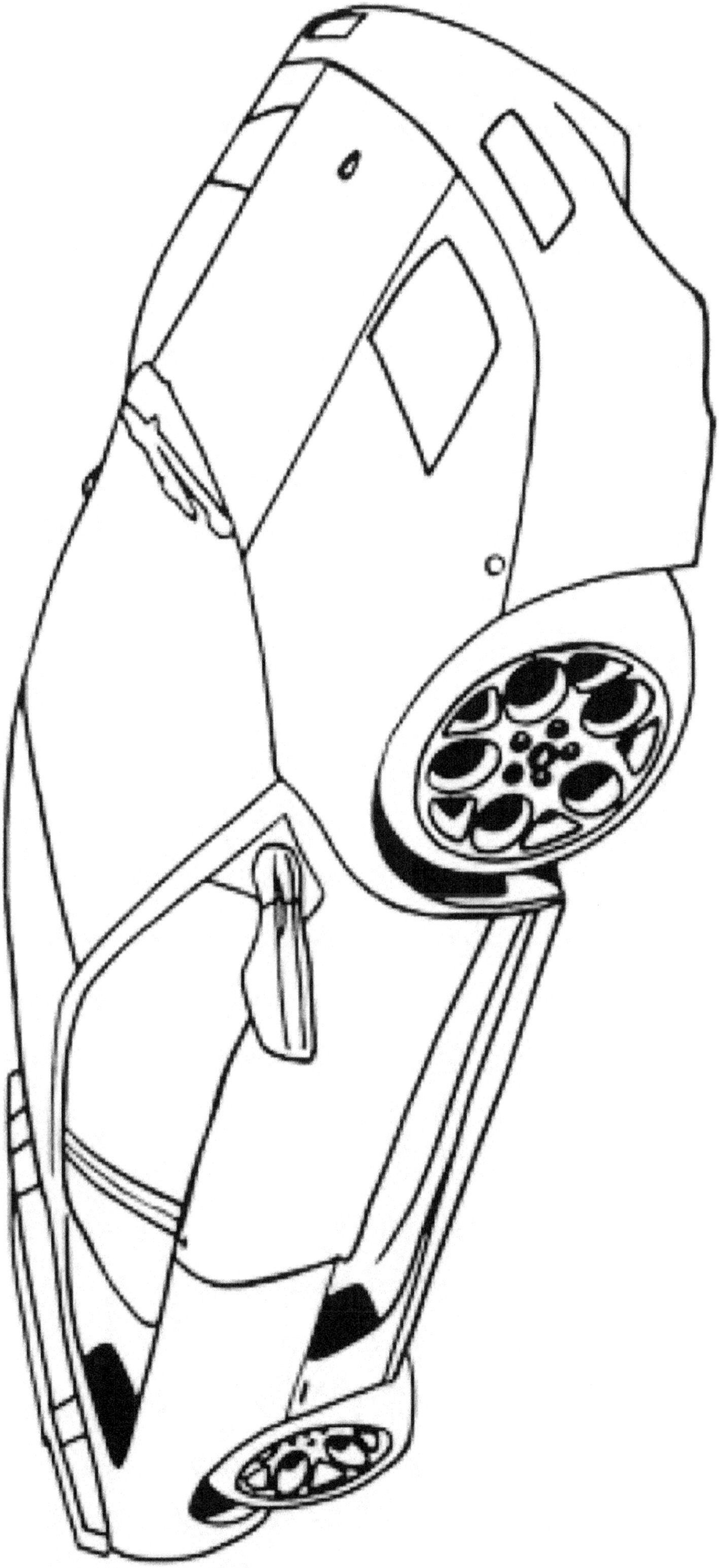

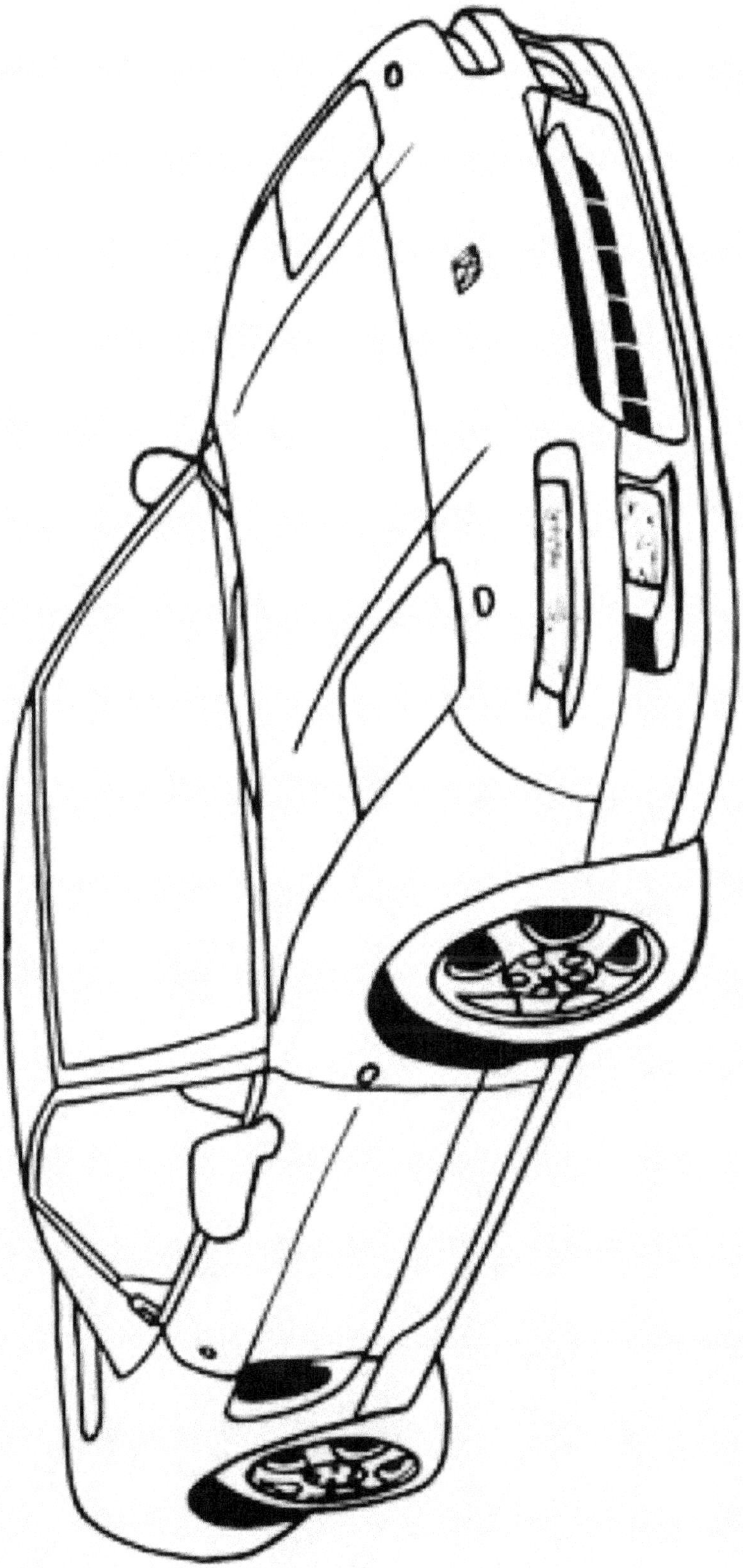

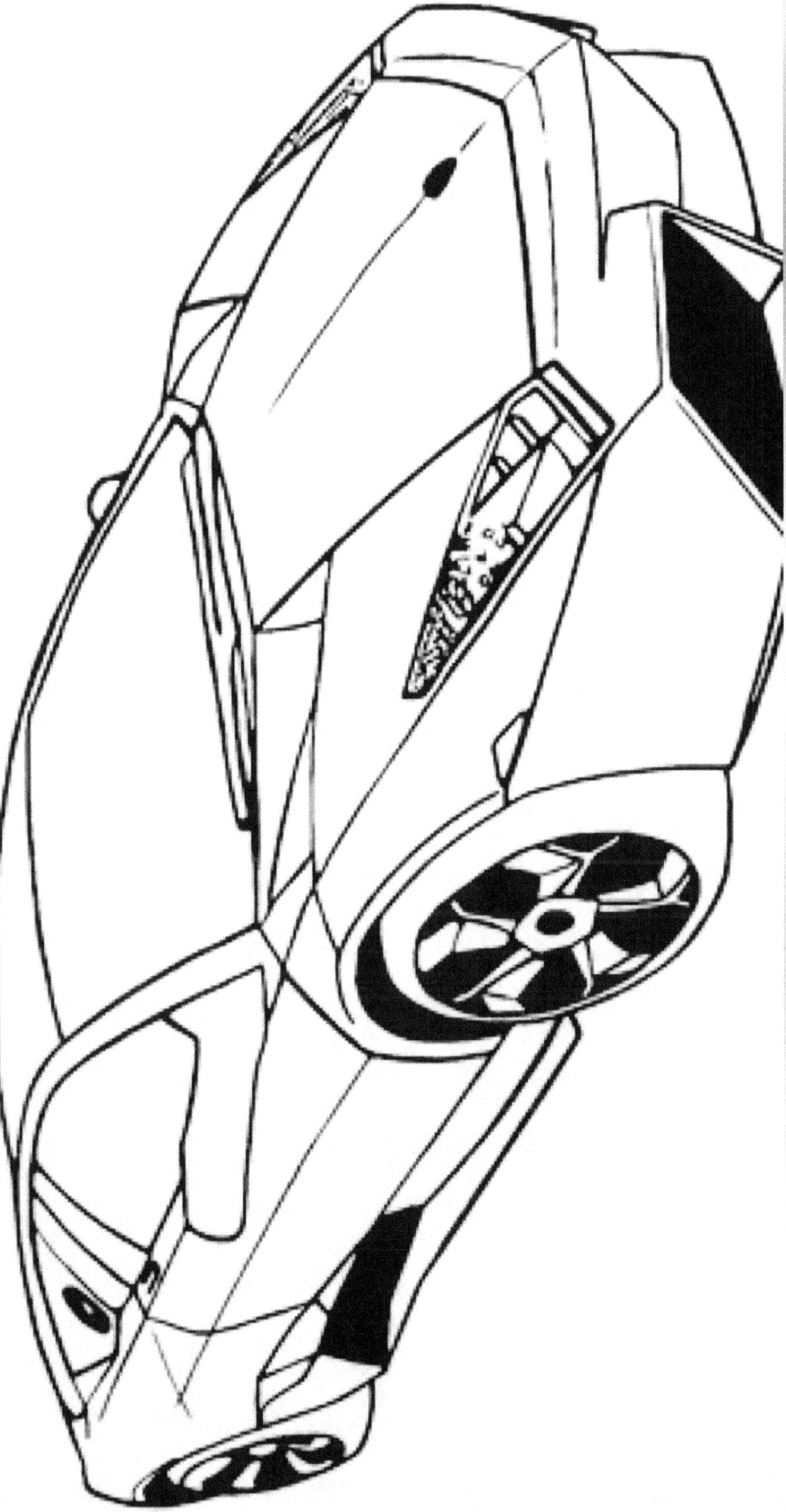

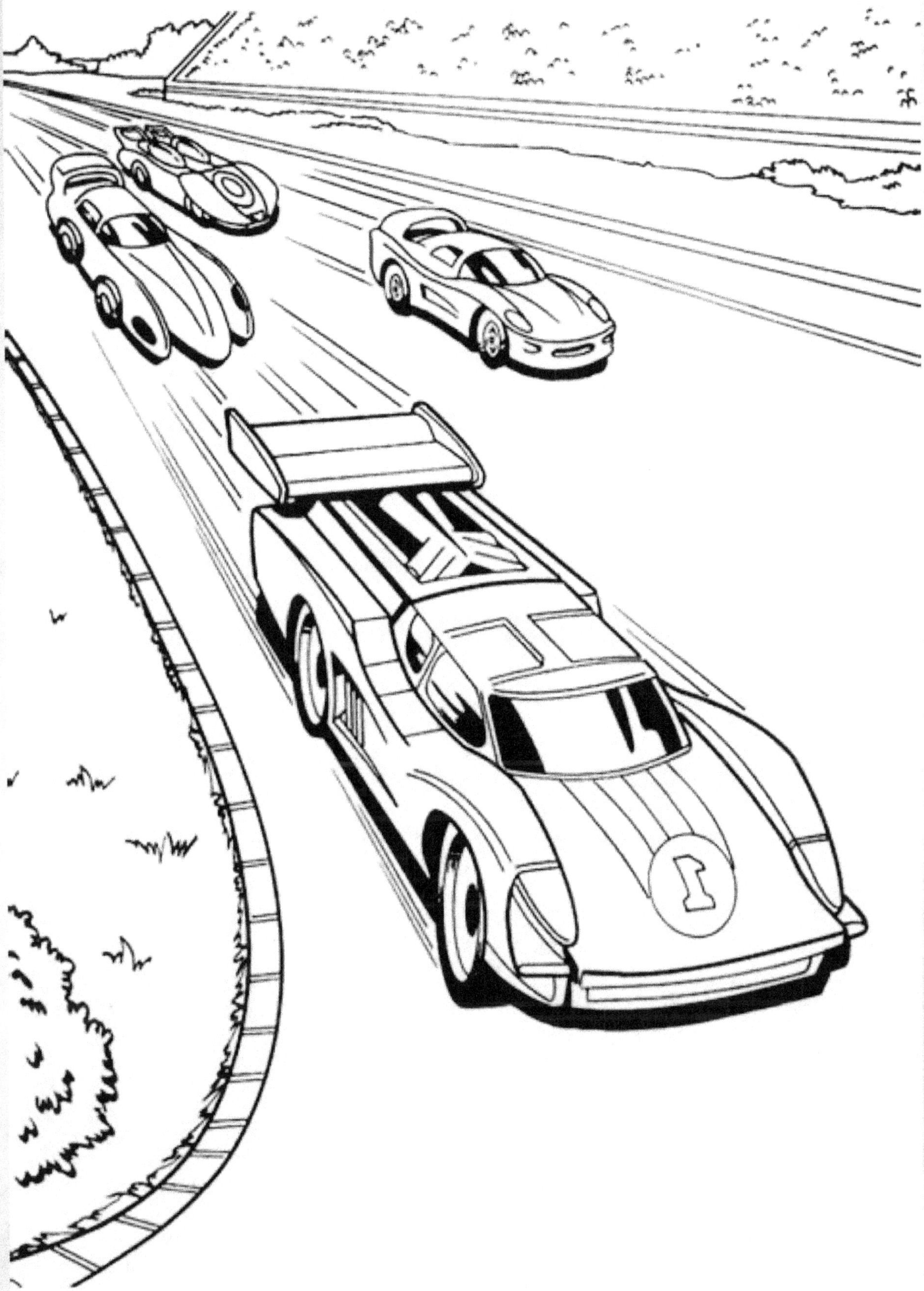

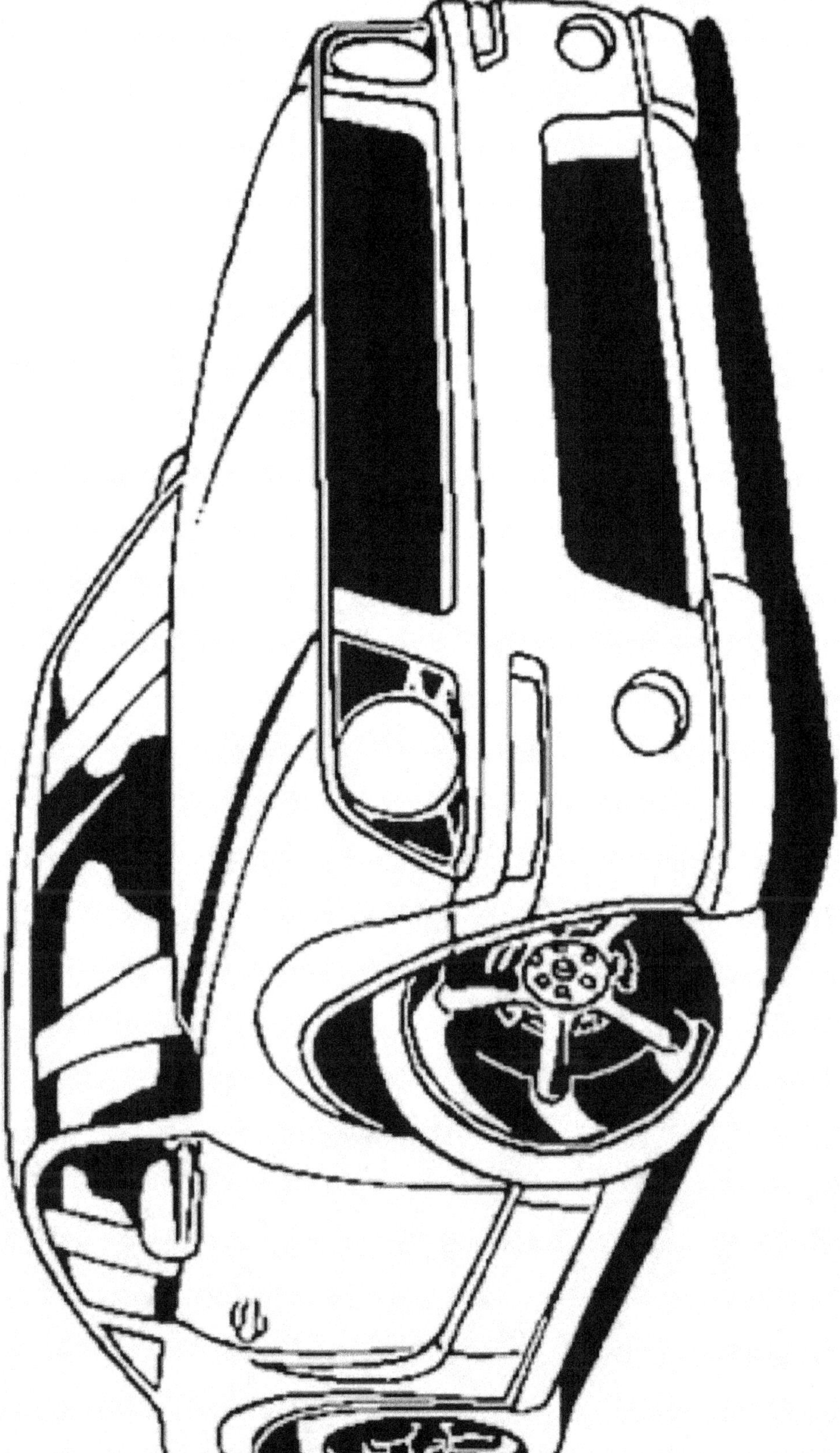

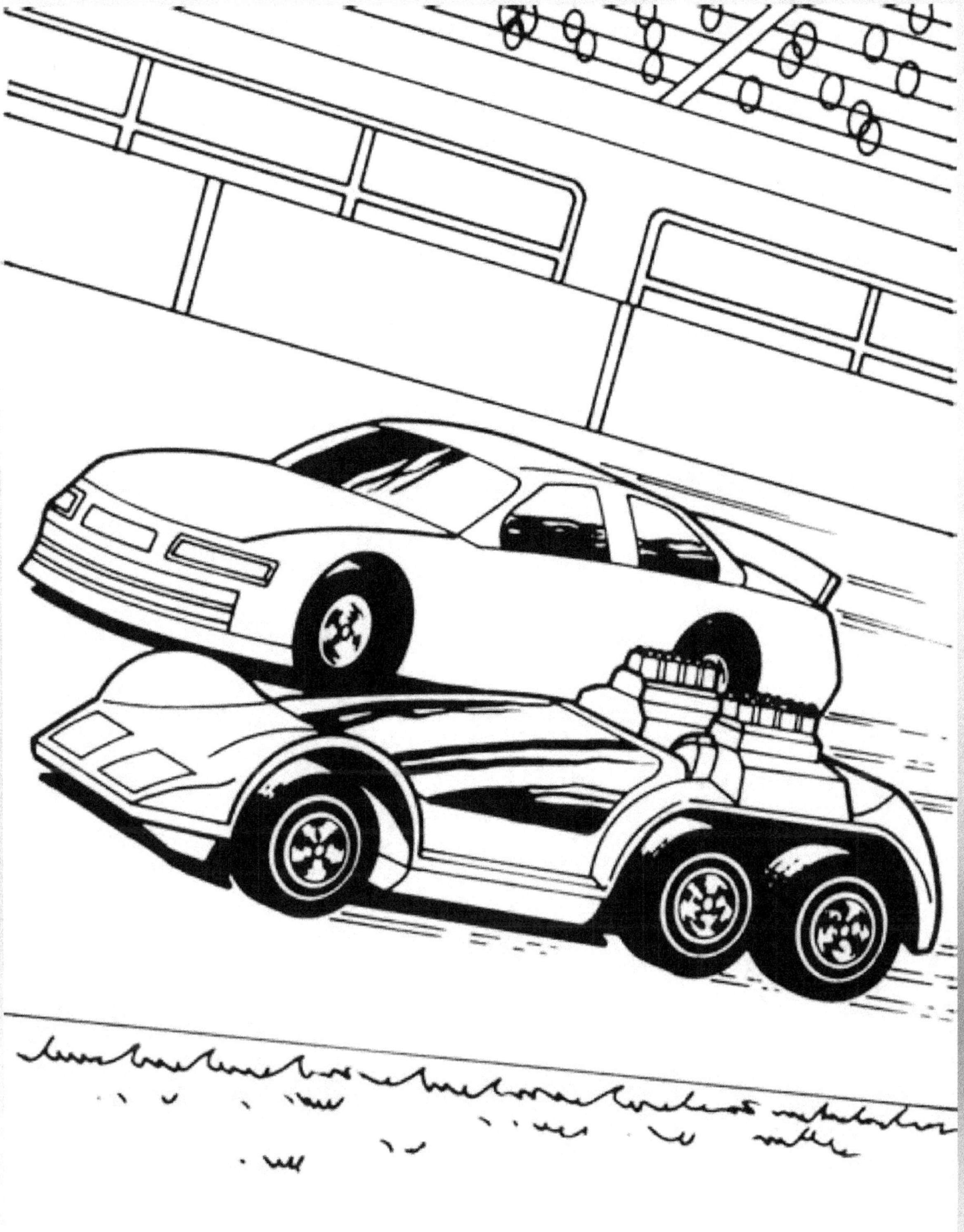

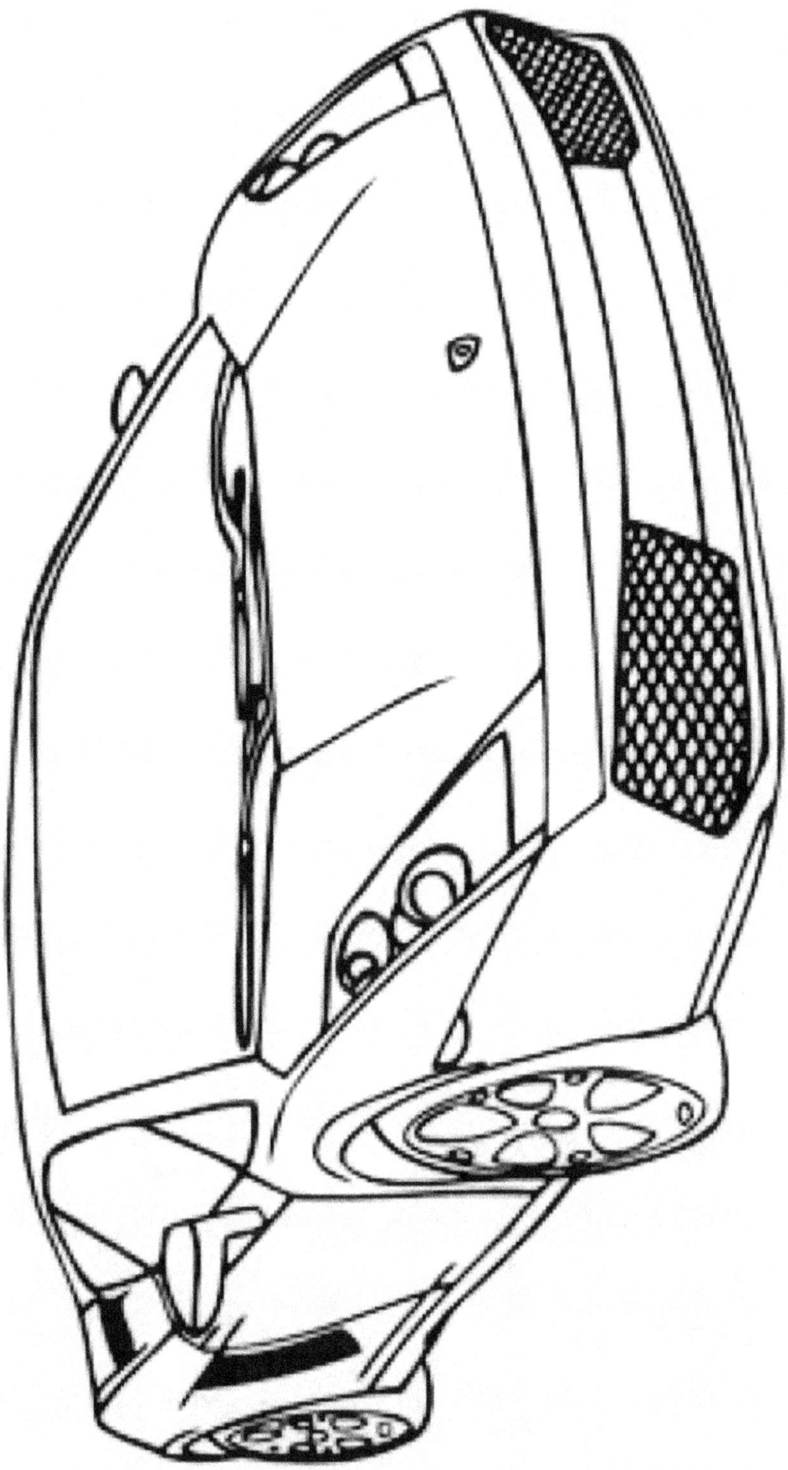

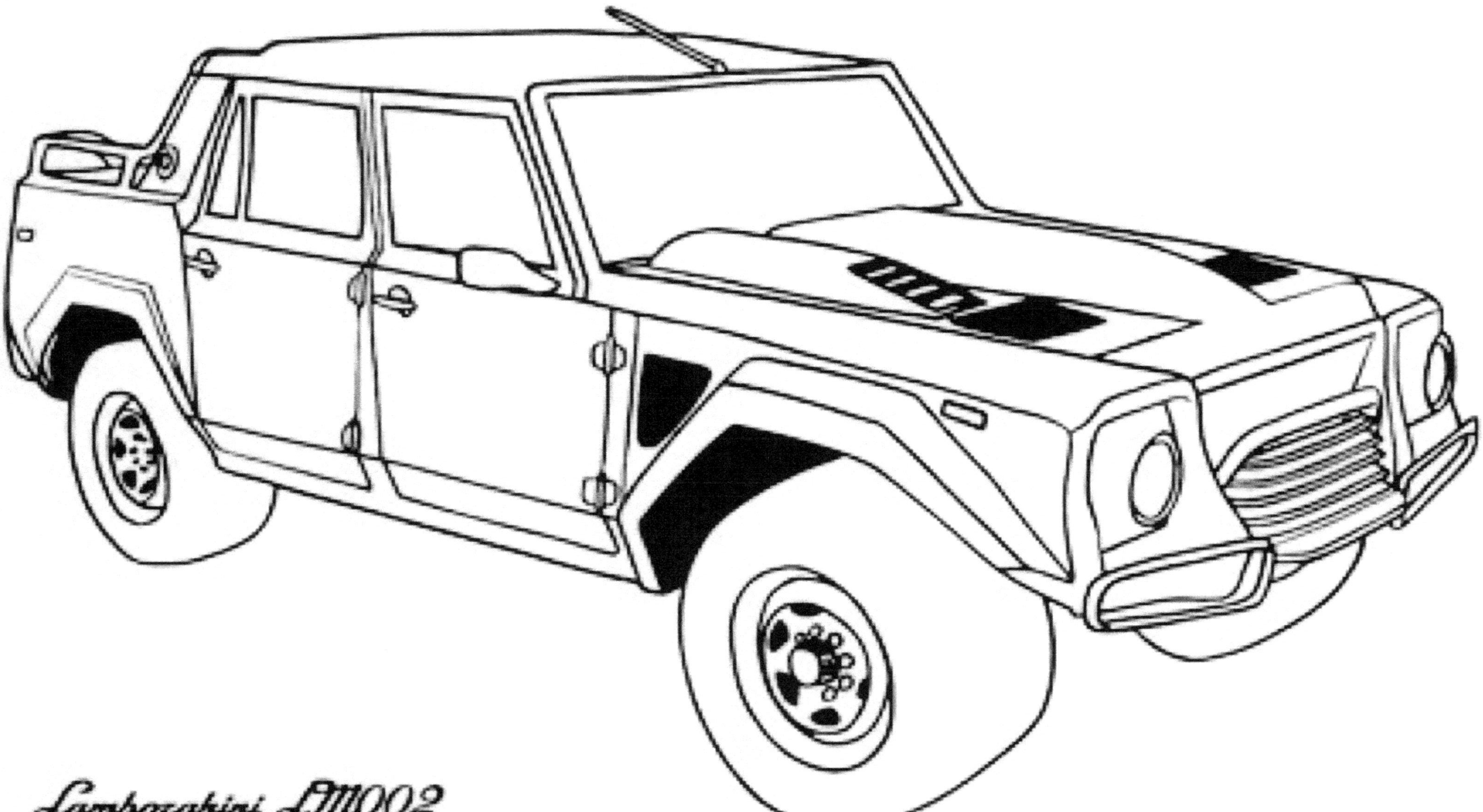

Lamborghini LM002

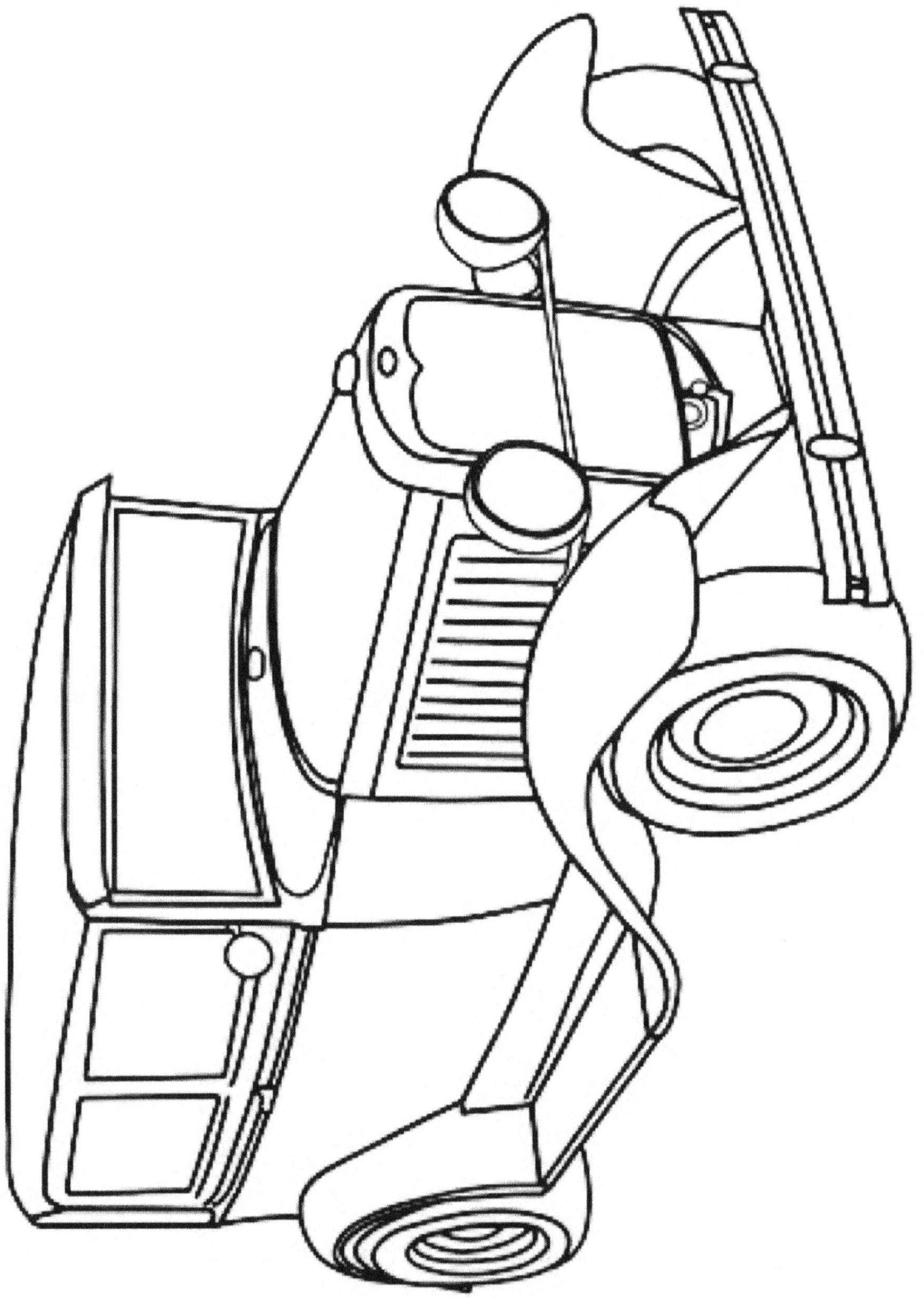

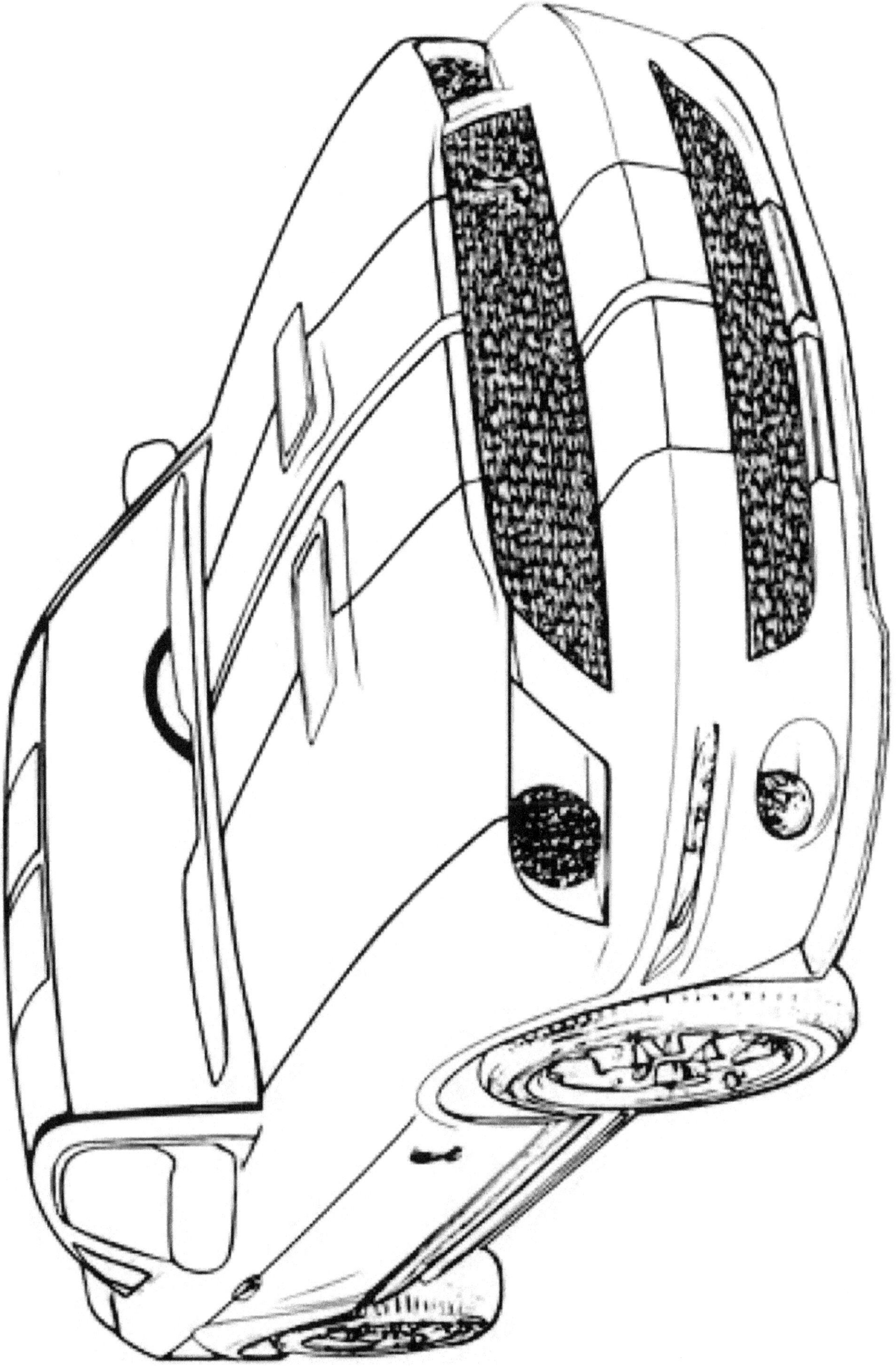

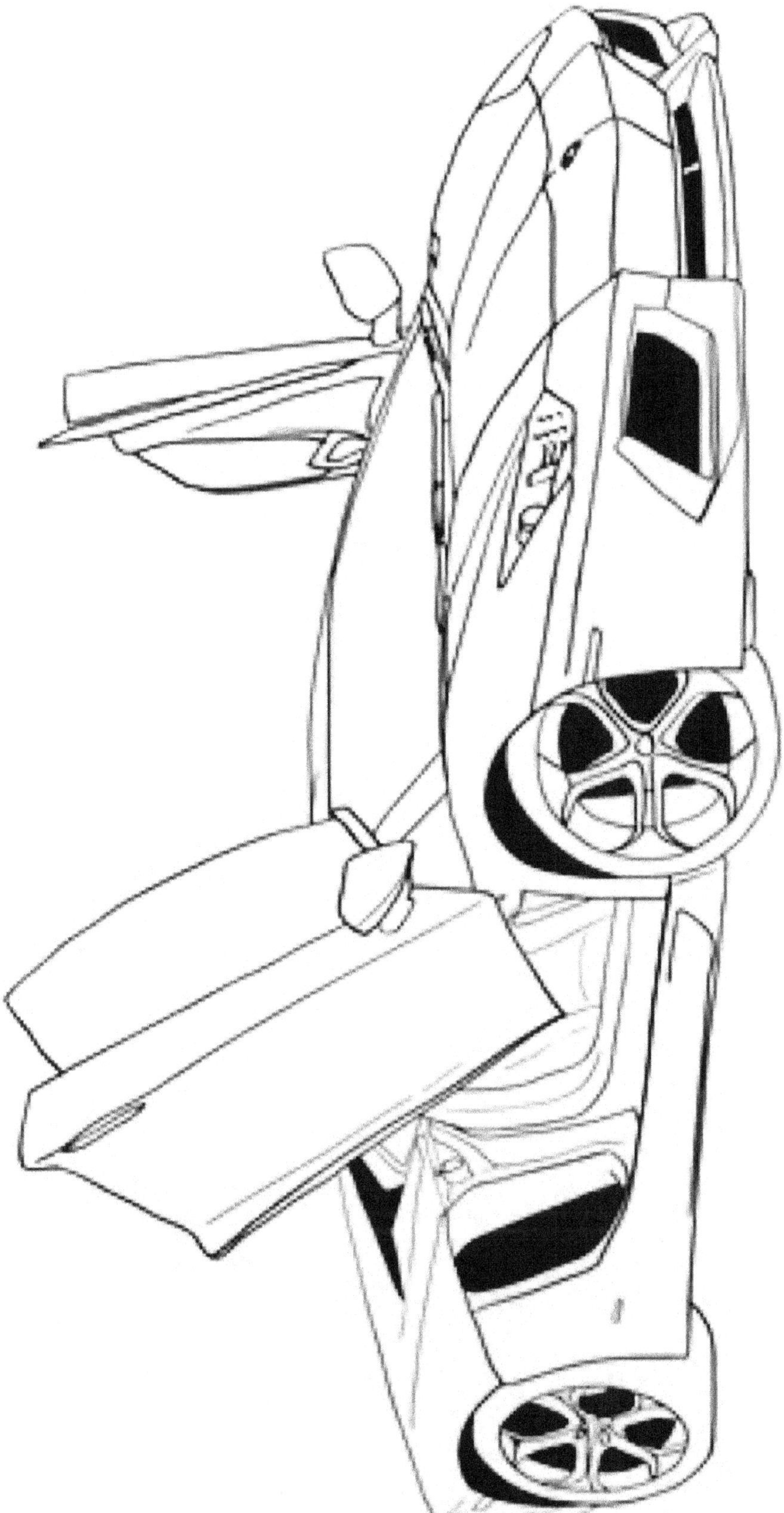

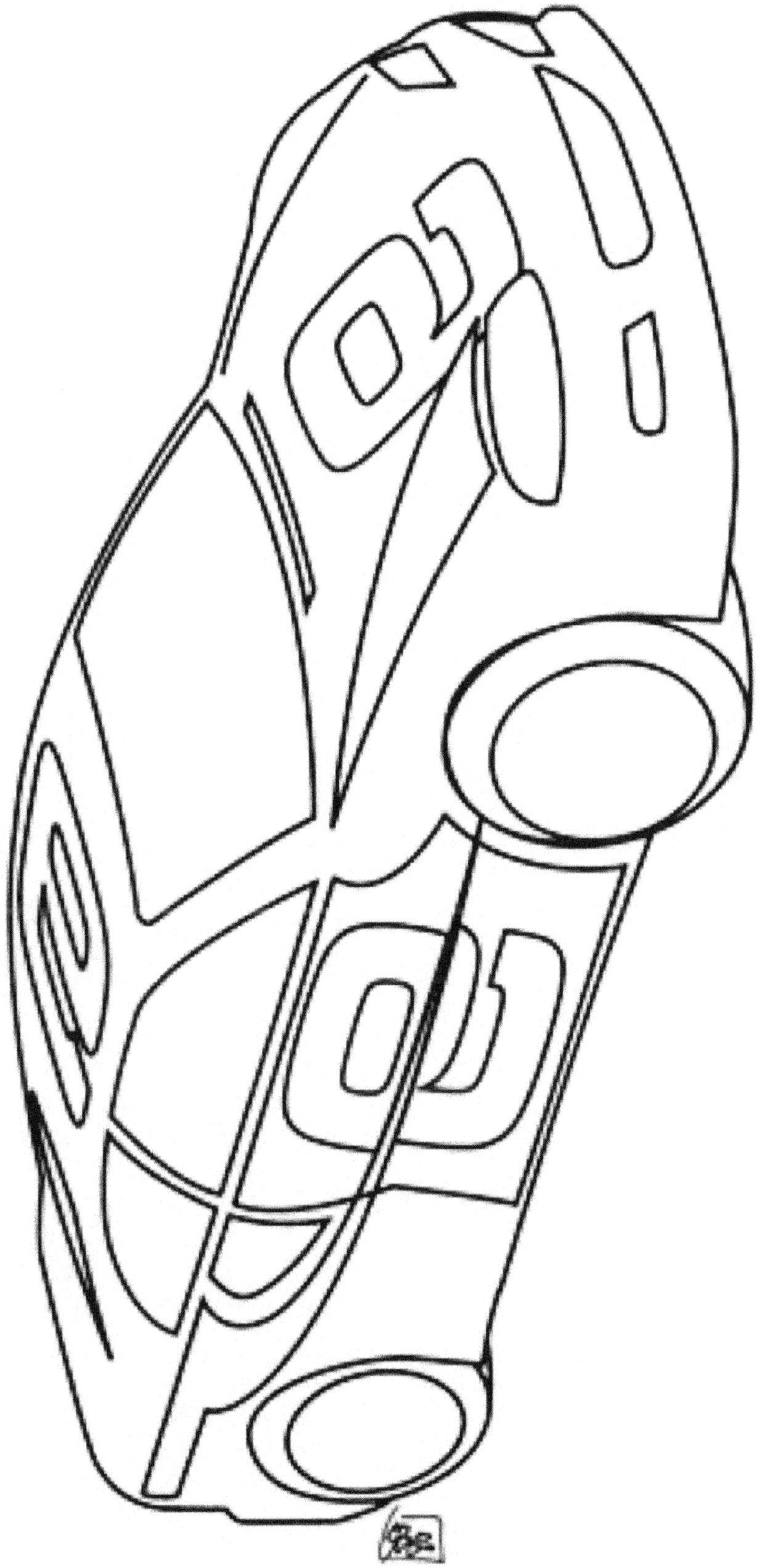

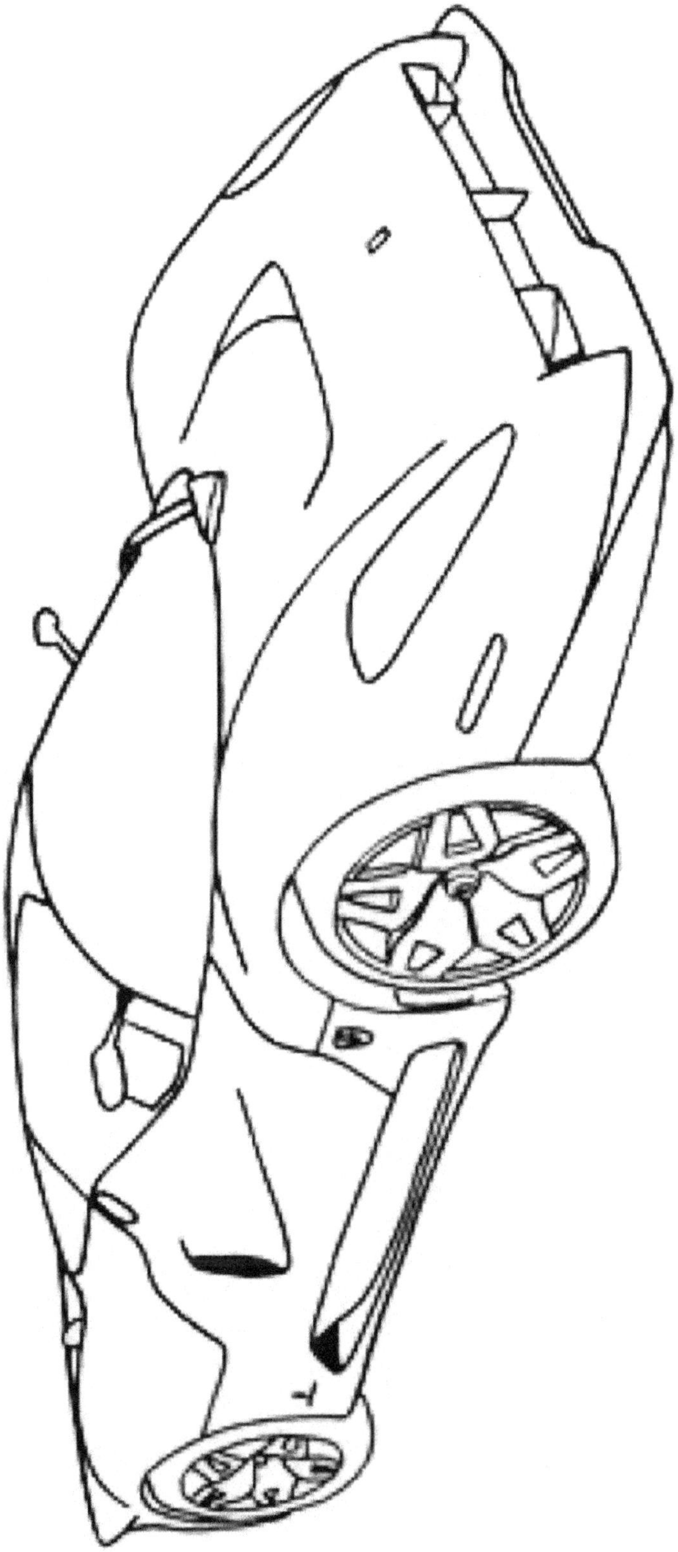

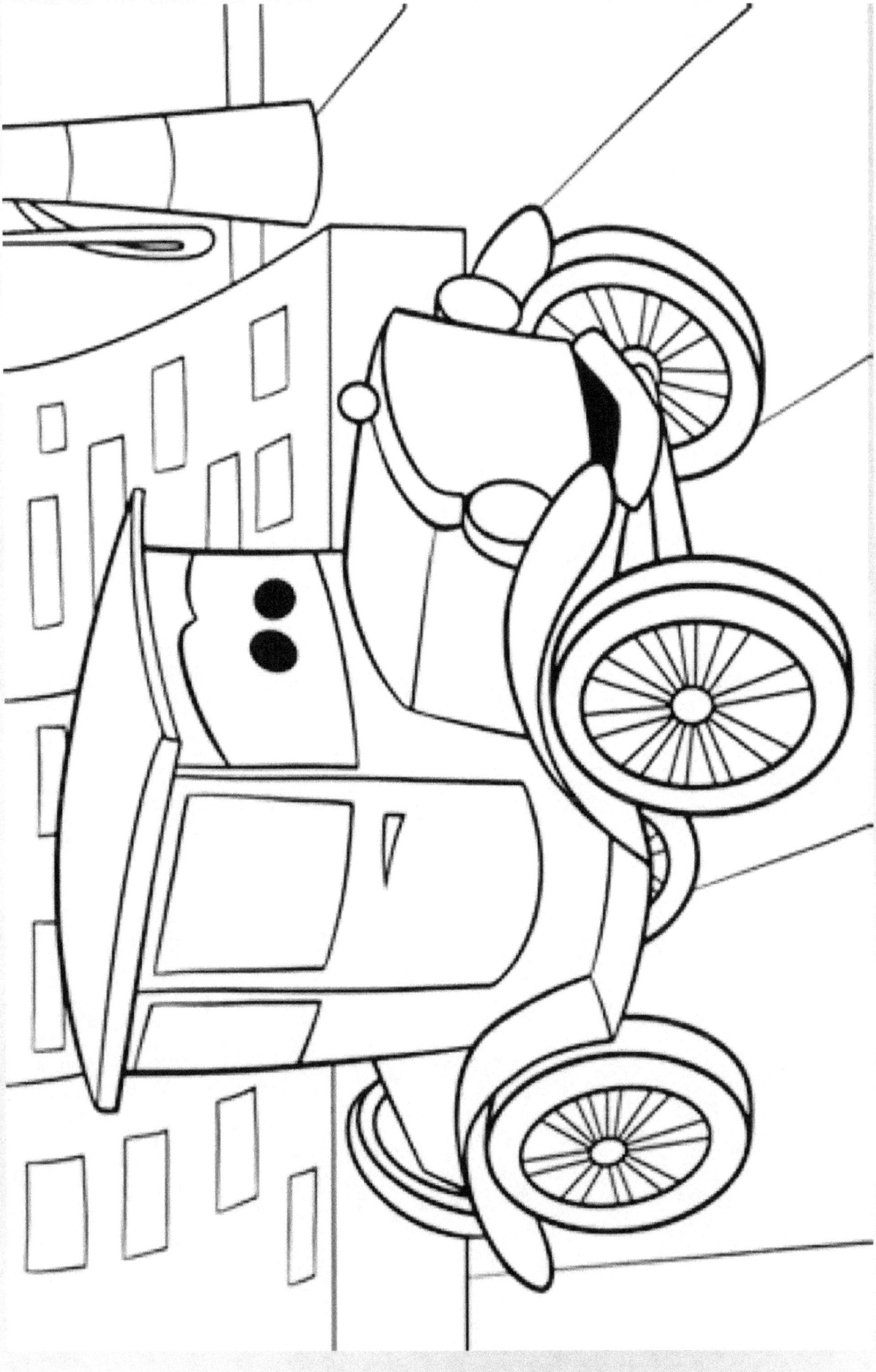

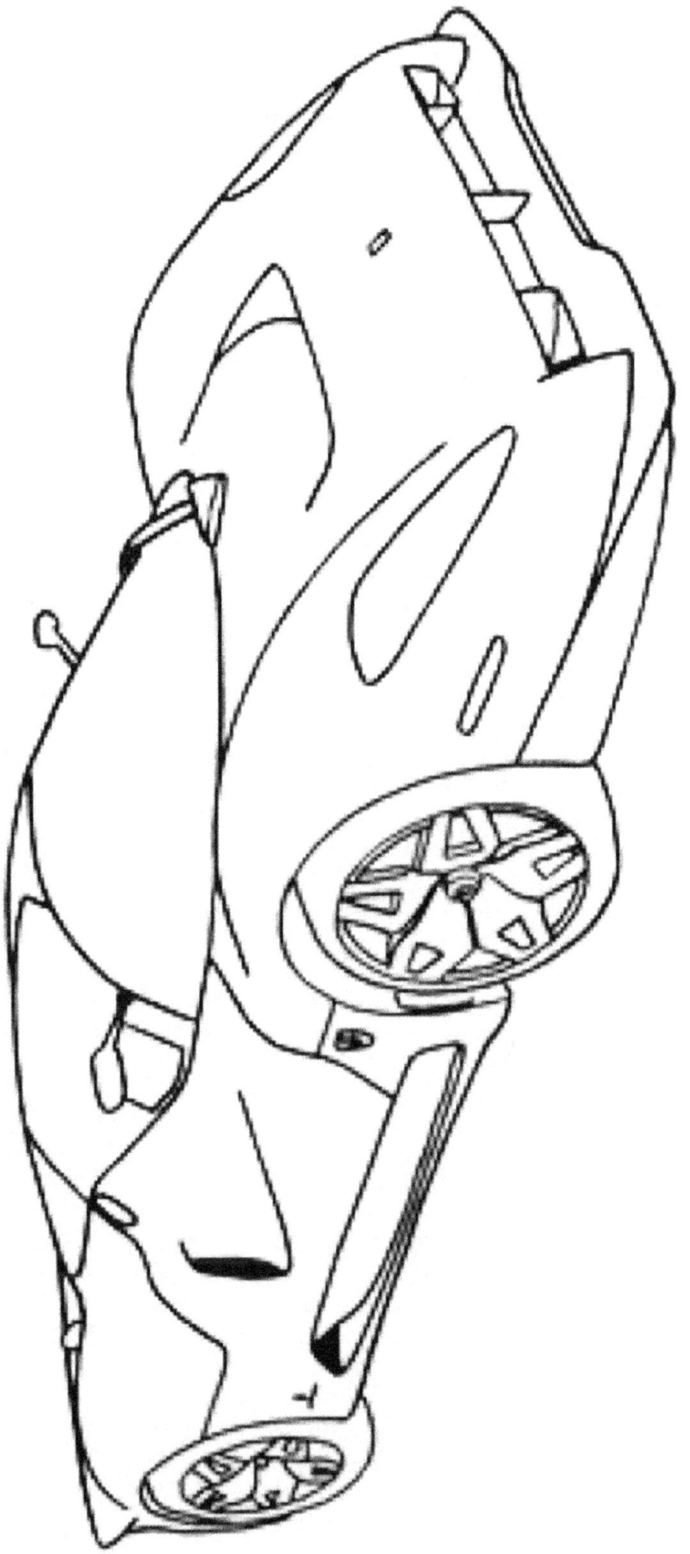

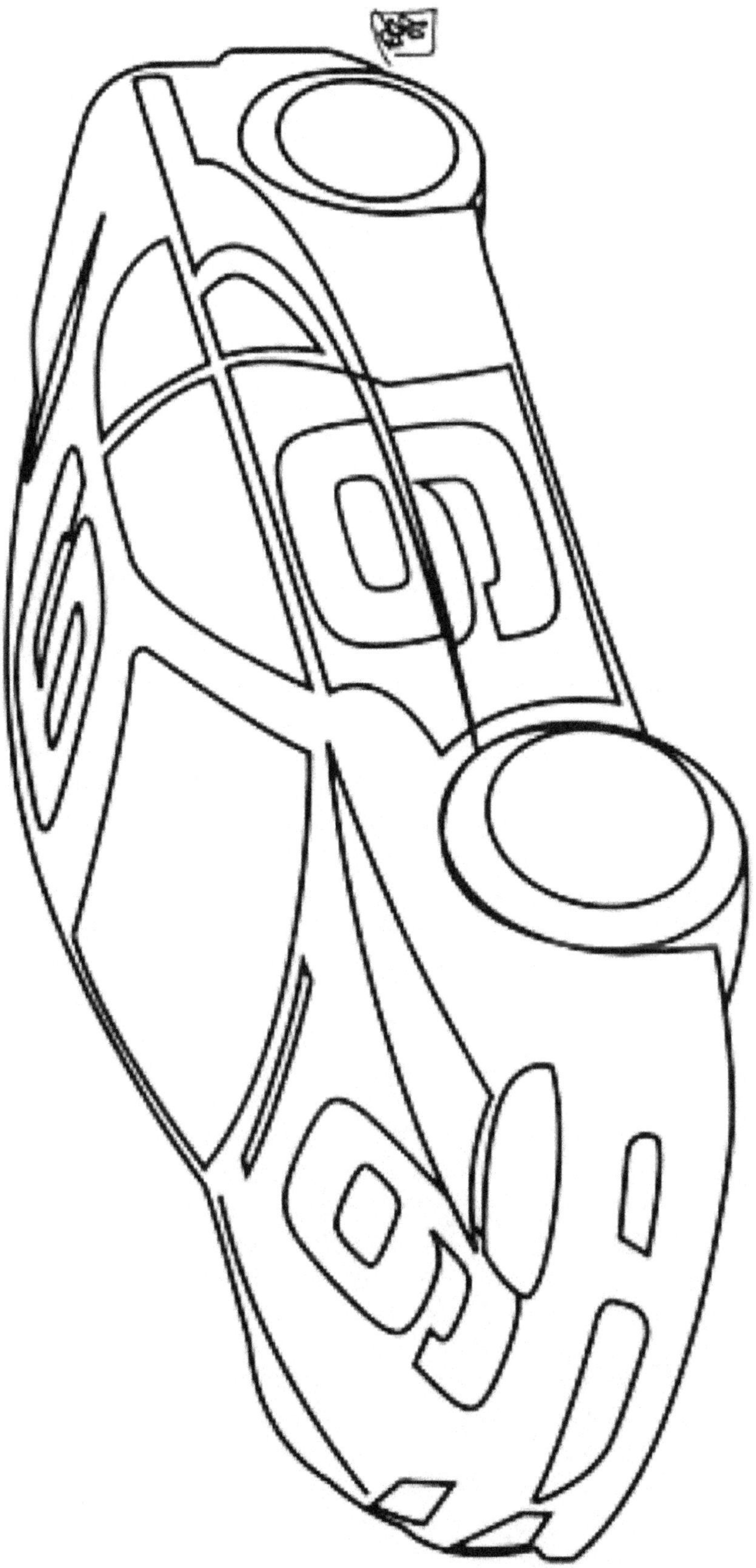

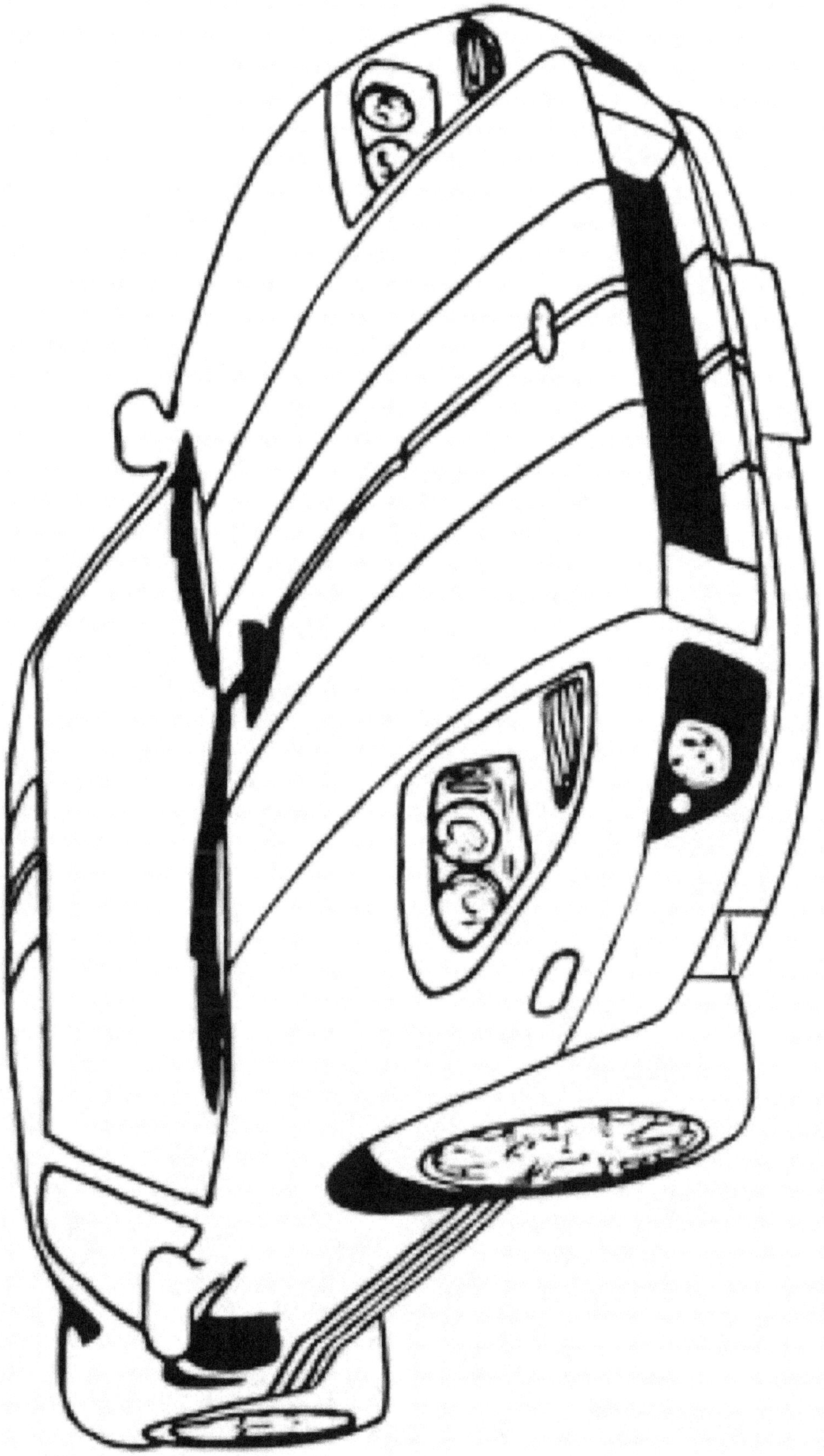

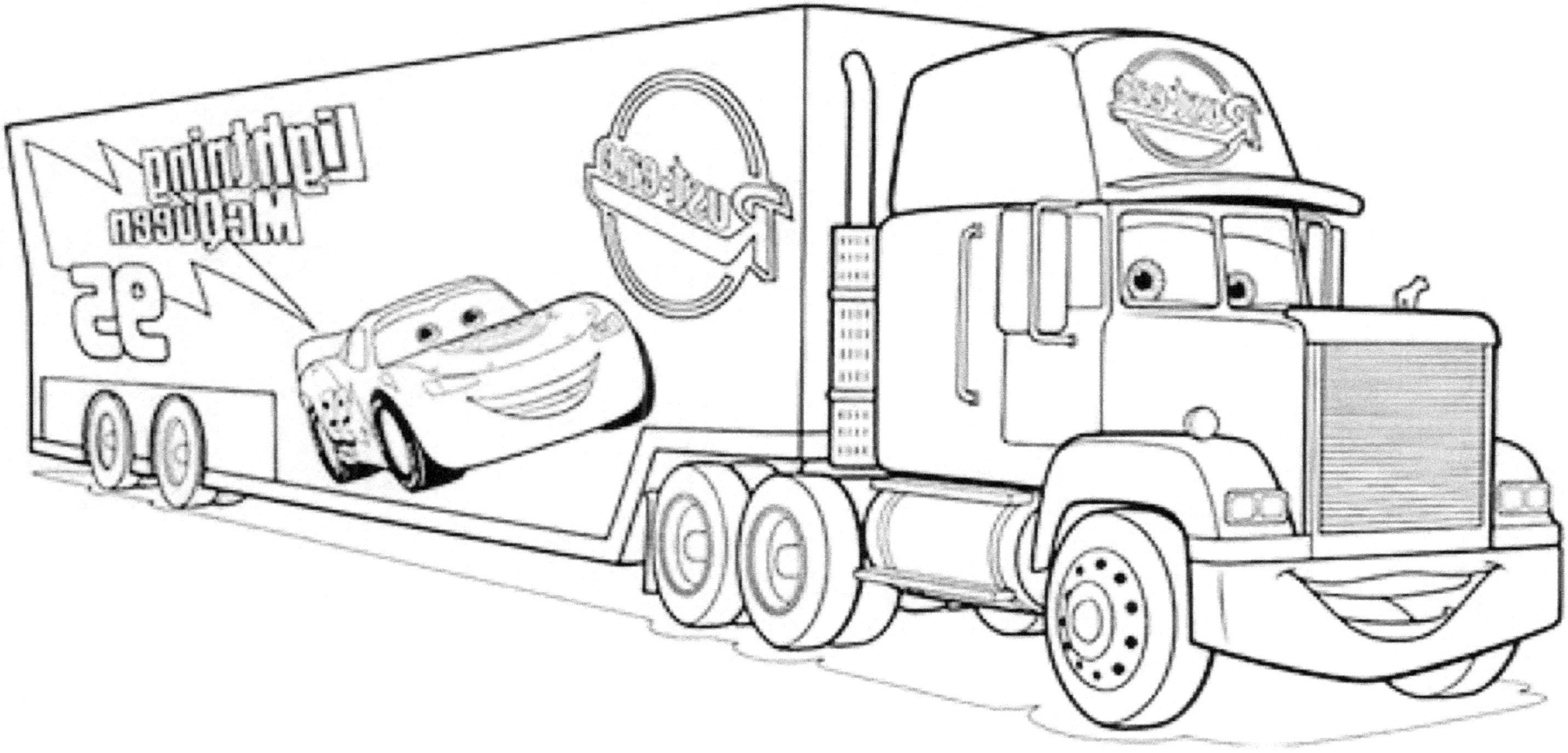

Lightning McQueen
95
Rust-eze
Rust-eze

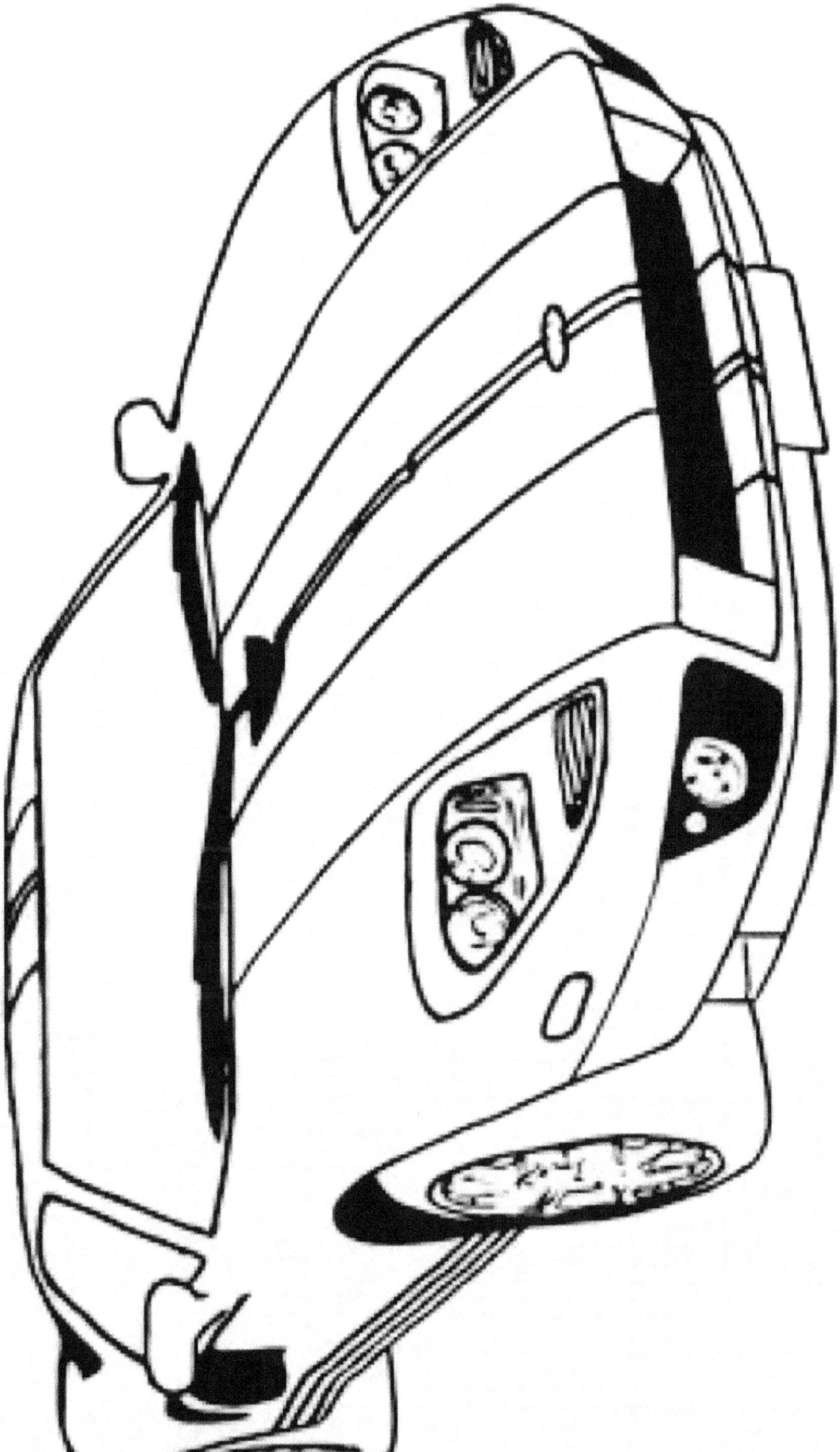

www.ingramcontent.com/pod-product-compliance
Lightning Source LLC
Chambersburg PA
CBHW082224290526
45794CB00009B/3667
* 9 7 9 8 8 6 3 8 3 9 9 4 3 *